STUDIES IN THE PERSONAL
SOCIAL SERVICES NO. 5

General editors: OLIVE STEVENSON and MICHAEL HILL

SPECIALISATION IN SOCIAL SERVICE TEAMS

Studies in the Personal Social Services

1 SOCIAL WORK AND MONEY
   by Michael Hill and Peter Laing

2 CHILD ABUSE: ASPECTS OF INTERPROFESSIONAL CO-OPERATION
   by Christine Hallett and Olive Stevenson

3 SOCIAL WORK WITH ELDERLY PEOPLE
   by Cherry Rowlings

4 SOCIAL SERVICE AREA TEAMS
   by Phyllida Parsloe

Specialisation in Social Service Teams

OLIVE STEVENSON
*Professor of Social Policy and Social Work,
University of Keele*

London
GEORGE ALLEN & UNWIN
Boston   Sydney

First published in 1981

This book is copyright under the Berne Convention. All rights are reserved. Apart from any fair dealing for the purpose of private study, research, criticism or review, as permitted under the Copyright Act, 1956, no part of this publication may be reproduced, stored in a retrieval system, or transmitted, in any form or by any means, electronic, electrical, chemical, mechanical, optical, photocopying, recording or otherwise, without the prior permission of the copyright owner. Enquiries should be sent to the publishers at the undermentioned address:

GEORGE ALLEN & UNWIN LTD
40 Museum Street, London WC1A 1LU

© Olive Stevenson, 1981

British Library Cataloguing in Publication Data

Stevenson, Olive
   Specialisation in social service teams. –
(Studies in the personal social services; no. 5)
1. Public welfare – Great Britain
2. Social services – Great Britain
I. Title   II. Series
352.94'4'0941

ISBN 0-04-362045-0
ISBN 0-04-362046-9 Pbk

Set in 11 on 12 point Times by Alan Sutton Ltd, Gloucester
and printed in Great Britain
by Biddles Ltd, Guildford, Surrey

The main aim of the series is to shed light on key areas of concern for the organisation and practice of social work in local authorities. The books are designed for practitioners and for social work students.

The idea for a series of this kind came about from our concern to secure wider discussion of issues which arose during a study of field work in social services departments. This project, funded by the Department of Health and Social Security, the Scottish Social Work Services Group and the Northern Ireland Department of Health and Social Services, was directed by Olive Stevenson and Phyllida Parsloe. Its main findings were published by HMSO in *Social Services Teams: The Practitioner's View*. None of the books in this series directly duplicates that report, but some of the issues in them were first discussed there and some of the data quoted in them emerged from that research and may have been reported there.

Olive Stevenson
Michael Hill

Acknowledgements

This book is the product of continuing discussion spanning five years with colleagues who have been or still are associated with our Social Work Research Project. I am grateful to them all but would mention two in particular. First, Sandra Strachan, who worked with me on the preparation of the chapter of our research report dealing with specialisation. Secondly, Rowena Gay, who has helped more than anyone else by her scrutiny of the journals and her meticulous care in the preparation of the manuscript.

As the Introduction indicates, I also owe a debt of gratitude to CCETSW for the original impetus for this work.

This book is dedicated to my aunt, Hilda, who is always interested.

Contents

Acknowledgements	*page*	8
Introduction		11
1 The Background to the Debate: Genericism Upheld		13
2 The Issues in Context		29
(*a*) Professional and educational		29
(*b*) Organisational		35
3 The Notion of Expertise		48
4 The Organisation of Work (I)		60
(*a*) The patch system		60
(*b*) Aspects of interprofessional co-operation		74
5 The Organisation of Work (II)		84
(*a*) The structure of teams		84
(*b*) Need for specialisation as perceived by social services departments		95
(*c*) Special interests of workers		101
(*d*) Skill development		102
6 Boundaries and Connections		111
7 Drawing the Threads Together		131
8 Some Implications for Education and Training		137
Bibliography		152
Index		157

Introduction

In 1973 I was invited by CCETSW to prepare a paper for their Curriculum Development Panel on the implications of the reorganisation of the personal social services for the education of social workers, with particular reference to the generic/specialist issue. I accepted and then found myself unable to fulfil my undertaking. When I settled down to the task it was befogged by uncertainty and lack of information about trends in the field. This led to an application to the DHSS to undertake a study of social service teams, which began in 1974. This threw much light on many aspects of team functioning and of the perspectives of those who worked therein, and some preliminary thoughts on specialisation appear in the report of that study (1978).* It became clear, however, that whilst one could not theorise about the issue without a thorough understanding of the actual workings of teams at present, this understanding did not of itself provide answers to an extremely complex question.

In this book I have begun to examine specialisation from a number of angles, all, in my view, crucial.

First, there are knotty theoretical problems concerning the meaning of terms often used imprecisely. What *is* generic, what *is* specialist in the contexts with which we are concerned? And can there be a recognisable entity – a generic social worker?

Secondly, the professional, educational and organisational history must be understood to make sense of our present scene. Although the account here is sketchy, it seems of fundamental importance to acknowledge that social services departments in the 1980s have a history and that this history has a bearing on what has and has not been done.

Thirdly, the case for the development of specialist expertise within social services departments is argued.

Fourthly, the organisation of work – itself a form of specialisation – is considered along six dimensions: the patch

---

*This research is henceforth referred to as 'our research' and is noted in the Bibliography under DHSS, 1978.

system, interprofessional co-operation, the structure of teams, the need for specialisms perceived by social services departments, the special interests of workers and the development of special skills.

Fifthly, some boundaries and connections are explored, that is, the 'grey areas' in which the relationship of social work to the service offered is not yet clear as, for example, in 'welfare rights'.

Chapter 7 is a bold, some may say foolhardy, attempt to provide one model of a social service team in which all the variables discussed previously as being relevant to specialisation are given some weight. The danger of so doing is that the model will be given undue prominence when the intention is to illustrate one way of reconciling the complex and seemingly incompatible elements necessary for good service delivery. If the model stimulates argument and alternative strategies, above all if it encourages experiment, it will have succeeded in its purpose.

The last chapter deals, somewhat cursorily, with some implications for education and training. Although some of it is related to the proposed model, a central point concerning the crucial importance of systematic staff development holds true for any developments in specialisation.

The book is solely concerned with one aspect of the team's functioning. It should therefore be taken as complementary to that of Phyllida Parsloe, who in *Social Service Area Teams* (1981) has examined other significant aspects of team functioning. It is particularly important to consider her observations on the dynamics of team relationships in connection with any development along the lines proposed here. Nothing will succeed if it cuts across the grain of the individual motivation and aspiration of team members. As Parsloe stresses, the importance of the team leader in creating a climate which is flexible and yet safe can hardly be over-emphasised.

Chapter 1

The Background to the Debate: Genericism Upheld

This book is intended to clarify some of the issues which underlie the present debate about specialisation in social services departments.* However, perhaps because of the upheaval, organisational and professional, of the last ten years, there is a tendency to ignore the history of what one might simplistically style the 'generic/specialist' controversy. This debate, lively in the interwar years in the USA and the UK since the 1950s, has profoundly influenced the development of British social work (Younghusband, 1978).

It is important to place our present concerns in this historical context, not only because of the sense of proportion that such reflection often brings but also because it shows how semantic and professional confusion, unresolved at the point of the 'Seebohm reorganisation' (Seebohm Report, 1968), have left us with no clear set of concepts or even guidelines upon which to base contemporary developments.

Furthermore, as will be argued in the last chapter, in focusing in this book upon specialisation there is no intention to deny the desirability and possibility of a generic basis for social work education. That, of course, hinges upon identifying and agreeing that there is a core of knowledge and skill which social workers hold in common, a difficult and contentious issue to which I shall return. If the reader will for the moment accept that premise, it is apparent that, although the educational implications are profound, it does not preclude some degree of special concentration by students; nor does it prevent us from the consideration of specialism in practice. What it can do – if

---

*Throughout, this phrase will be used to include social work departments in Scotland and health and social services boards in Northern Ireland.

we have the intellectual energy and stamina to follow it through – is to free us from past definitions of specialisation and to create new ones, perhaps better fitted to the problems of the time and to our indigenous agency structures.

It might help us to have a moratorium on the word 'generic' for a few years; it has meant many different things to many people. As Timms (1968, pp. 27–8) points out, there has been a basic confusion over the root of the word:

> If, for example, we take 'generic' to mean 'general' then the complementary term would be specialised. Adopting this definition has particular implications. It involves us, for instance, in thinking in terms of the general social worker, on the one hand and the specialist on the other. If, however, 'generic' is used in the sense of genus, we are led to think in terms of a common name covering a number of species. In this use of the 'generic specific' idea, a 'generic social worker' as a kind of person like the 'general social worker' mentioned above would not be conceivable; the term 'generic' would refer to those characteristics which make it sensible and convenient to call social workers in different fields by a common name.

Timms (p. 29), wittily but misleadingly, goes on to draw a portrait of the so-called 'generic' social worker, an expert in human relationships and needs, 'moving from problem to problem like an eighteenth-century noble, at home everywhere because he is always with the same kind of people'. Clearly the social worker cannot move here and there without additions or modifications to a professional repertoire of knowledge and skill: the question is whether there are common elements underlying practice which make the job recognisably the same and which make movement between different fields of practice feasible. I would wish to argue that this can be so and that it has been demonstrated by the competence of many social workers who have moved 'from problem to problem', not because 'they are always with the same kind of people' but because the processes and objectives of the task are basically similar. Butrym (1976, p. 75) takes Timms's point further: she writes of the very fundamental difference between conceiving of generic as 'general' . . . or as . . . 'genus' . . . The former interpretation might encourage the acceptance of an emphasis on 'the lowest common denominator' in order to ensure that everybody learns the same – a practice which is bound to have disastrous results on the intellectual standards of social work. The view that 'generic' means 'in common' must result, on the other hand, in a recognition that there is no inherent incompatibility between 'the generic' and 'the specific' but that, on the contrary, the two are complementary and interdependent. General concepts, such as those of loss or deprivation, for example, can only become truly meaningful in a specific context such as loss of income or health, deprivation of freedom or affection.

But perhaps such argument obscures rather than clarifies. Perhaps the distinction which Timms draws, and Butrym supports, is not as clear as it at first sounds. If there is a 'genus', or 'species', called 'social worker', this means they have something in common. Unlike herbivores or aphids, their commonality lies not in what they eat but in what they do. Thus, up to a point (and this is an important qualification), they are able to 'do the same' in respect of a wide variety of persons and situations, that is, the *genus* can perform as *general* social workers. The phrase 'lowest common denominator', which Butrym uses, is misleading if it is used in its popular sense which is denigratory. The specialist will on occasion possess knowledge or skill the generalist does not have. It will be seen in succeeding chapters, however, that client problems and needs are not – and could not be – mirrored by specialisations which somehow ensured a perfect fit. Therefore, it is part of the skill of the generalist to assess the particular aspect (or aspects) of a client's problems which requires specialist advice or intervention, and part of the organisation's responsibility to attempt to provide them. The analogy of the general practitioner in medicine is pertinent, especially since, in recent times, the *specific* skill which he should have in diagnosing and treating his patient as 'a whole man' has been stressed.

Semantic confusion has been further compounded by the three different ways in which the term 'specialist' has been used. The first two came from across the water and refer to *fields of practice* ('settings') or *methods of social work*. The third, more home grown, refers to client groups. Although 'fields of practice' and 'client groupings' may have much in common, they are not the same. Hospital social work is a clear example. Hospital social workers work in the same 'field of practice'; even when one has separated the physical from the psychiatric, however, it is apparent that hospital social workers who work in 'physical' hospitals serve a range of clients whose problems are extremely diverse, and whose only common ground is that of illness or disability (even that does not accurately subsume maternity wards!). The clients of hospital social workers are of all ages; their stay in hospital may be of any length of time; their problems may be sharply focused upon illness or the illness may be simply the presenting problem which reveals others, unconnected with illness. To compare this work with, say, that of Family Service Units or the special units of the NSPCC shows that hospital social work cannot be credibly sustained as a specialism based upon a client grouping. The 'field of practice' is more convincing, since it can be argued that the distinctive nature of the activity lies in the agency context in which it is practised and, above all, in the interprofessional collaboration which is integral to it. Even that, however, can lead us into difficulties. For it will be argued in later chapters of this book that interprofessional co-operation and collaboration should be key issues in determining specialisation in social work in the community, outside the hospital ambience. This has become much clearer in the last five anxious years of inquiries into the non-accidental deaths of children (Hallett and Stevenson, 1980).

What gives hospital social work its distinctive flavour (and brings relief to those who move from 'generic' work in area teams) is, of course, in part a chance to put some boundaries round work at a point in one's career. (It is also a relief to many social workers that the responsibility for the patient's state of health is firmly in the hands of the doctors, whereas in 'community care' the position is often blurred.) Most hospital social workers work for units or firms, defined by the clinicians, or for groups of wards and educators. In his paper Goldstein (1973, p. 21) set out his views on the 'generic' argument: 'Practice . . . is very specific and highly individualised. What is generic is the knowledge base that undergirds the range and array of professional actions that the worker employs.' He suggests (p. 29) that 'a unitary approach . . . is an attempt to arrange a set of variables that have both distinct and related characteristics into a related whole . . .' and offers examples of 'social learning' and 'problem solving' models as a means of achieving that. Pincus and Minahan also address the same issues. They argue that a generalist is, paradoxically, a kind of specialist. They spoil their case by exaggerated and imprecise language, for example, when they state that a generalist 'is a specialist because of his rare concern with the total ecology of the problem and the persons involved' (p. 35). But let us not throw out the substance with the rhetoric. An important point is made, which will be further developed in this book, that a generalist is a kind of specialist in putting pieces together and seeing how they relate. The same claim can, of course, be made for a general practitioner in medicine.

Vickery (1977, p. 58) concludes:

> Both Goldstein and Pincus and Minahan emphasise the importance of social problem definition and the assessment of where, within accessible social systems, intervention is required. This is the hallmark of the unitary approach and is in marked contrast to practice that is guided by the size of the client system . . . or with the problem or pathology it presents . . . However, even with a common methodology, the question remains of how to organise knowledge about people, problems, situations, systems and their inter-relations, for responsible action towards a specific end.

That is the nub of the problem. There is no doubt that these unitary theories have had an impact on British social work education. Beguiling as they may be to social work teachers, they do not solve the problem of the acquisition of skills across a broad area in basic training of one or two years' duration. What they do is to free workers to examine a problem and choose models of intervention more flexibly.

They also have more far-reaching implications in the approach to problem-solving which requires a wider view of the client/environment constellation than that formerly encouraged by 'choice of method'. How much they do so in practice is as yet uncertain, partly because of the time it takes for such approaches to 'filter through', partly because there are factors in agency expectations and structures which may make it difficult for the enthusiast for 'integrated methods' to pursue his ideas. That a beginning has been made, however, is illustrated by articles such as that of Bywaters (1978), a practitioner in the social services, and the work of Currie and Parrott (1980) which is considered in Chapter 4.

In short, therefore, we can see that the words 'generic' and 'generalist' have meant differing things to different people. This, combined with continuing doubts and debate about the nature of social work itself, has seriously obscured the argument and impeded professional development. It is humbling, and worrying, to read Towle's paper given in 1956 to the (British) Association of Social Workers, 'Generic trends in education for social work'. It is apparent that many of the issues she addressed so cogently then are still unresolved (although it should be noted that Towle's thesis rested upon casework and did not encompass the other modes of intervention which we have been discussing).

Towle (pp. 1–2) reiterated her belief that social work was about

> effecting change in the interaction of individual and situation . . . Thus one factor of social work is the range and variety of stress situations which the worker must be prepared to recognise, analyse and with which he must attempt to deal. Furthermore the social worker is . . . expected to see the inter-relationships of the different stresses.
>
> The current trend . . . is toward the acceptance of the intermediary or integrative role . . . [The earlier mistake was to equate] *the generic with the elementary and the superficial and conceive of the specialised as* ipso facto *being advanced and profound* [my italics]. It was due in part . . . to the fact that we had not delineated what we needed to know in order to perform in diverse settings in relation to a variety of stress situations.

The main proposition in this argument, that it is a mistake to equate the generic with the superficial, is one with which the present author would agree and seems to represent a point of disagreement with Timms (1968) and Butrym (1976), and agreement with Goldstein (1973) and Pincus and Minahan (1973). It is also a challenge to those whose arguments for specialisation in social services departments rest upon a similar assumption. What has been missing and is still incomplete, as Towle said in 1956, is a series of theoretical linkages which rest generic social work upon a sound knowledge base, a point to which I shall return later. The thrust of my argument, however, is that social work can be enriched by both generic education and generic practice, since they can and should facilitate the transfer of knowledge and skills across problems and situations. The fact that there are forces working against this in our social services departments does not vitiate the argument. Nothing in this book should be taken as an encouragement to go backwards to the earlier fragmentation, professional and organisational, of social work, which would occur if basic training were to revert to specialisation – as we see already happening in the Certificate of Social Service – or if there were no room for generic social work practice within social services departments. On the contrary, the findings of *Social Service Teams: The Practitioner's View* (DHSS, 1978) that there was a large amount of informal specialisation by qualified social workers within the area of families and children was a source of concern, not only because of the different *levels* of social work skill available to other client groups, but also because there was little evidence of imaginative transfer of knowledge, even by supervisors who had been generically trained.

It is argued that we proceed best from a base of genericism. What does that imply?

In my view, Bartlett (1970) has provided the most coherent and well-argued thesis in support of the view that social work has begun to lay a common foundation and has pointed the way to its consolidation. Bartlett (p. 37) insists on the importance of generic knowledge-building but, in considering 'barriers to integrative thinking', refers to 'anti-intellectual attitudes'. She points out that social workers, in stressing the uniqueness of the individual and his problems, have been resistant to the process of generalisation which is indispensable to theoretical development. 'It is not recognised that reality itself is a chaos of detail, that facts and experience alone will never reveal their own meaning' (p. 39). Whilst it is customary for professions to borrow for use, social workers have run into particular difficulties in so doing: 'finding security in one cluster of theory . . . they concentrated excessively on such a single body of knowledge.' 'It is the thesis of this discussion that such fragmentation of knowledge will continue to occur until recognition of the essential elements in social work is strong enough to hold the profession more together' (p. 71). Such an approach does not imply that the presentation of different disciplines is somehow 'emulsified' (Stevenson, 1971), although the extent to which integration is attempted will remain a matter for debate. It does, however, imply that, overall, there should be a purposeful choice of knowledge from other disciplines related to the professional activity. Bartlett does not, however, underestimate the knowledge derived from social work experience which suggests that the formulations we need to make should be about 'the behaviour of people under stress, the meaning of the situation to them, their efforts at coping, their ways of seeking and using help . . . all of which fall within the particular experience of social work' (p. 75). Bartlett suggests (p. 203) that 'the next important and greatly needed step would seem to be to identify a small number of concepts and generalisations that would be so related as to be integrative for the profession'. She further refers to 'misuse of the democratic approach', suggesting, although these are not her words, that social workers have been reluctant to accept intellectual authority. 'Each group wants to make a fresh start. Unfortunately, this tendency devalues and ignores a need for continuity and consistency of thinking over a long enough period to demonstrate results . . .'

It seems that, in British social services departments, there has been a kind of collusion between workers and employers to produce an 'anti-intellectual' stance. Fears of elitism, of authoritarianism, a lack of commitment to the intellectual component of social work activity have conspired with agency norms and values which, in general, do not ascribe high status to educational attainment, to produce a situation which stimulates *neither* generic *nor* specialist development in terms of knowledge-building.

Nor have educators, until recently, done much to redress the balance. For example, their record in social work research has been weak. (The reasons are complex and this is not said unsympathetically.) Where research has been undertaken, it has tended to be individualistic and *de novo*, thus confirming Bartlett's point that we lack a systematic programme of knowledge-building, in this instance, of research. Again, there are many reasons for this which cannot be explored here; they are as much structural (for example, related to research funding arrangements) as personal. But we are left with a somewhat alarming situation in which the cry goes up for specialisation without the certainty of the base upon which it is to develop.

It is the elements which might form this base which Bartlett examines. She takes as her starting point a definition of social work activity which is not dissimilar to that of Towle (1956), cited earlier, and one which will find favour with most social workers in Britain today. With a focus upon social functioning, Bartlett suggests that the social interaction between 'people coping' and 'environmental demands' is the key point for social work intervention. Once one begins to explore the implications of this apparently anodyne statement, its complexities and potentialities begin to emerge. She suggests (p. 100) that it 'has the possibility of providing what social work has never had – a concept broad enough to encompass the profession's scope and yet clear enough to provide a focus that will stimulate integrated thinking and effort'. It enables us, for example, to study the environmental component, 'the people who comprise the environment', including other professionals. In Bartlett's view (and my own) both direct and indirect service to the client, that is, work *with* and *for* him, are an essential part of social work intervention. Vickery (1977, pp. 43–6) refers to the debate in the USA between direct and indirect service. In my view, this was sterile and did not reflect the real nature of good practice. Social work must embrace the polarity and work with it. Bartlett (p. 132) writes:

> In their practice, teaching and writing, social workers have been influenced by ideas that are divisive rather than integrative. Furthermore they have used ideas that are not necessarily opposites as if they were alternatives and choices must be made between them. [For example] . . . cause and function . . . generic and specific . . . individual and community . . .

She quotes Ausubel (though in a different context):

> 'The pseudo issue underlying the controversy . . . can only be eliminated by specifying in more detailed and precise fashion how the interaction takes place and the relative weight of each factor in determining the course and outcome.'

This discussion of the debate about 'genericism' may seem a long way from our theme of specialisation in social service teams. But to move to specialisation without it is like trying to grow branches without the tree-trunk.

The level of generality concerning the nature of social work has, so far, been high and somewhat abstract. Yet the idea of an attempt to understand the factors which affect the social functioning of persons under stress, and seek to alleviate them, enables social workers to take from other disciplines for their own purposes and to contruct a knowledge base from which to operate generically. It is here that it is apparent how much more work we have to do. Bartlett rightly cites human growth and behaviour sequences as an example of an area in which social workers, in borrowing, have constructed something unique for their own use. But another area she mentions, that of 'crisis theory', is open to more questions as to whether its assumptions, so widely accepted by social workers, have been adequately tested empirically to justify the weight placed upon them.

In concluding this chapter, I propose to take one of the

most usual of the 'linking themes' in social work, that of loss, to illustrate both the possibilities and difficulties of identifying the common knowledge and its application in such a concept.

All social workers encounter clients suffering from loss or deprivation and from anxiety, rational and irrational, about prospective loss. This may be of many kinds, for example:

loss of intimately loved persons, through death, separation (psychological and/or physical);
loss of cared-for persons (typically the multiple losses of old age);
loss of 'faculty';
loss of home, whether forcibly (e.g. eviction) or by choice, albeit perhaps ambivalent (e.g. admission to an elderly persons' home);
loss of social roles/status (e.g. divorce or unemployment);
loss of material comforts.

The question to be addressed is what these losses have in common and in what ways their impact differs upon the people who experience them. Loss or deprivation by definition is *diminishing* of the person who suffers it. That which one had and valued has been taken away. It is, therefore, universally experienced in some degree as a threat to one's very existence, an 'ontological anxiety', and is reacted to by depression sometimes masked by anxiety. The extent to which these emotions dominate or conflict with others is, of course, variable. Feelings of relief, even of exhilaration, may be present in many situations of loss, in bereavement, divorce, or unemployment, for example. Much depends on whether the experience generates new opportunities or is experienced as offering at least in part a better quality of life. Yet to deny 'the loss factor', even in more hopeful circumstances, and the depth of its inner meaning to individuals, is to miss a vital ingredient in the complex package of emotions centred upon such common human experiences. The mother may mourn the loss of her baby as her son goes to school whilst she is still rejoicing that he is developing normally to adulthood.

All social workers therefore need to understand something of the psychic processes involved in such experiences, of the effects upon social functioning and social relationships. They can apply both psychological and sociological theories to such experiences. They also need, however, knowledge of the specific effects of certain types of loss. One of the attractions of Marris's (1974) *Loss and Change* to social workers is its attempt to link three totally different aspects of the subject, across different cultures, issues and disciplines. Marris examines bereavement, slum clearance and an aspect of the Kenyan business world. (The last, seemingly improbable, example concerns 'the loss of a sense of the meaning of life', p. 114, consequent upon the breakdown of the social structure.) Marris suggests that the

> sense of bereavement is likely to be provoked . . . where crucial purposes have been disorientated, either because an attachment has been broken or because circumstances are too baffling to attach any purpose to them or because purposes are brought into contradiction by the consequence of different aspects of life (p. 148). Recovery from grief depends on restoring a sense that the lost attachment can still give meaning to the present, not in finding a substitute . . . (p. 149). When we impose disruptive changes on ourselves or others, we need to allow some kind of moratorium on other business, so that people can give their minds to replacing the thread of continuity to their attachments . . . (p. 150). The whole purpose of change may be aborted by the mishandling of loss (p. 151).

Such statements, although dealing generally with loss, and not exclusively with bereavement, carry echoes of work by Bowlby (1969, 1973 and 1980), Parkes (1972) and others. They are meaningful to most social workers in many of the situations in which they are required to intervene. Provided (and it is an important proviso) that they do not become dogma but are subjected to empirical testing as the opportunity arises, they offer a conceptual bridge which is experienced as a kind of intellectual relief. Something has been put together which needed to be put together. The pity of it is that during the years we have formally acknowledged genericism, both in education and in practice, we have done so little to develop these bridging concepts, even to the extent of relating for professional purposes work from different disciplines. It is outside the scope of this book to attempt it: but merely to mention other concepts, less often discussed than that of 'loss', is to remind ourselves what work remains to be done if we pursue our goal of improving our understanding of social interaction and appropriate intervention. Take, for example,

privation (as distinct from deprivation, what one has never had);
stress – its causes and manifestations;
individual and social mechanisms of defence.

Readers may add to the list; the question at issue is – would the systematic analysis of such concepts which move between the person and the environment give social work the generic knowledge base from which to move confidently into specialisation? Further, will the analysis of 'integrated methods' give us *a generic framework for intervention* which in no way precludes the development of individual specialisation by individuals, groups, or teams? Bartlett (p. 194) argues that our earlier so-called specialisation might more accurately be described as 'a profession growing through its parts'.

> It now becomes possible *and urgent* [my italics] to move ahead in eliminating the confusions that have persisted over so long a period. When specialisation has eventually been given its proper place in relation to the common base, then contributions from specialists will continually enrich it. (p. 195)

To use my earlier analogy, this book does not delineate the tree-trunk adequately before going on to describe the development of its branches. But this chapter has attempted to demonstrate that there is no fundamental incompatibility in a position which accepts genericism, in the sense of common knowledge and skills, whilst urging the need for specialisation along certain lines. That this is at present inadequately theoretically formulated cannot be disputed. But the magnitude of the conceptual task should not be underestimated. In the absence of an Einstein for social work, there seems to be a need for a kind of social work think-tank, a structure in which a group could work together, relieved of some of the daily pressures which fragment rather than integrate our approach. Whilst this will not convince the cynics, the reality of underlying genericism seems to me to have been well illustrated by the numbers of social workers who, in the past ten years more than ever before, *have* moved across fields of practice, client groupings and methods of intervention, often, typically, without articulating the common base that enables this transition to be relatively easy. To ignore this phenomenon, given impetus by professional and organisational change, is wilfully to 'conceal the evidence' before our eyes that there is a common perception of role and function upon which to build.

Chapter 2

The Issues in Context

(A) PROFESSIONAL AND EDUCATIONAL

The previous chapter has shown that the organisational changes in the personal social services in the UK in the 1970s did not take place in a theoretical vacuum. There was a protracted and, at times, heated debate on both sides of the Atlantic about these matters. Some idea of the complexity of the argument and of the consequent confusion surrounding the use of such terms as 'generic' and 'specific' has been given. In this chapter these theoretical matters will be put into the context, first, of professional and educational developments and, secondly, of agency function.

The movement to professional unification

Younghusband (1978) has documented the period leading up to the creation of social services departments in her detailed account of social work in Britain between 1950 and 1975. This shows the distinctive origins, value systems, theoretical frameworks and practice orientations of the major fields of practice whose claims to specialist expertise were so hotly debated in the period leading up to, and during, the first 'generic' courses in 1954 at the London School of Economics and subsequently elsewhere. It is not in the least surprising that medical social workers, psychiatric social workers, child care officers and probation officers, to name but four major groups, should have experienced grave doubts about compatibility within one professional association.

The resistance to unification was made up of many elements. There were real theoretical problems, some of which have been outlined in Chapter 1. But there was also resistance to change, especially when it was feared it would mean loss of occupational identity, of a highly significant reference group, and of certain professional values. These fears were not without foundation, as is shown by the subsequent troubled history of the British Association of Social Workers, partly focused upon the 'open membership' question and its association with unionisation.

Then there were the stereotypes each group had of the others. Stereotyping is a psychologically economical device. It involves the simplification of traits which in that process may become distorted. Yet there must be, as we say, 'a grain of truth' or the stereotype falls and there were distinctive characteristics to be joked about, criticised and admired within the occupational groups who eventually agreed to unite professionally. These reflected both selection and training, and the nature of the work.

The medical social workers, so the stories ran, were British, 'nice', precise and precious; the psychiatric social workers were Middle European, using their formidable intellects to attack intellectual defences, especially in students; the child care officers were busy, jolly but intense. And so on. These frivolous remarks serve to remind a younger generation of social workers, to whom some of this may seem remote, that the struggle for unification of the profession, coinciding as it did with proposals to unify local authority personal social services, involved people's feelings, values, attitudes and traditions. Nor should social workers be unduly apologetic. Malherbe's (1979, pp. 56-8) admirable discussion of issues surrounding accreditation includes a reminder of the lengthy and complex processes by which medicine, over the centuries, established itself 'generically' as a profession.

The momentum towards unification, however, continued to grow throughout the 1960s. The Standing Conference of Organisations of Social Workers (SCOSW) was set up in 1961; composed of eight professional associations it was, as Younghusband (1978, Vol. II, p. 169) remarks, 'a key point in the move away from specialisation and isolation towards identification of social work as a whole'. When the British Association of Social Workers (BASW) was formed in 1970, seven of the eight associations in SCOSW relinquished their separate identity. (Only the National

Association of Probation Officers stayed outside, although its members were permitted to join BASW.)

That these forces were irresistible seems clear – with hindsight. One of the most significant symbols was the creation in 1954 of a new journal, *Case Conference*, which ran alongside the various separate journals of professional groups and crossed the boundaries of fields of practice. As Younghusband (1978, Vol. II, p. 161) remarks, '*Case Conference* . . . was widely read in Britain and overseas and had more influence than other journals as a general forum for social work'.

Education and training before 1971
Interlocked with these developments were issues concerned with education and training, again ably analysed by Younghusband (1978). A curious and anomalous situation had arisen in the 1950s and 1960s. The London School of Economics in 1954 led the field in the provision of so-called 'generic courses' and, from this, others followed, often described as courses in 'applied social studies', in an attempt to provide education which would fit social workers to work in various fields of practice and, to a lesser extent, in different modes of intervention. The effect of such educational innovation, however, was hampered by two factors: first, separate finance and fragmentation of responsibility centrally; secondly, subsequent employment opportunities. The Central Training Council in Child Care, located in the Home Office, was first in the field with earmarked funding, from 1948, for courses for child care officers and residential staff and grants for students. Later, the Probation and After Care Department of the Home Office also sponsored courses and students for work in the probation service. Following the Younghusband Report (1959), the Council for Training in Social Work (the forerunner of CCETSW) sponsored (but did not fund) courses for non-graduates located in polytechnics and colleges of further education to train them for work in the health and welfare services. A separate course for medical social workers was run by the Institute for Medical Social Work until 1970; alongside that, medical social workers were

increasingly training on university generic courses, although grant aid for students was difficult to obtain. The psychiatric social workers retained some separate courses in universities. To summarise a muddle is difficult! The situation with which the newly formed Central Council for Education and Training in Social Work found itself confronted in 1971 was near-chaotic. The effects of course promotion, including financial aid, by various different bodies were far-reaching. Many of the tutors who were recruited to teach on such courses had had experience in those particular fields of practice, and sometimes had a powerful intellectual and emotional investment in meeting the educational and professional needs, as they saw them, of the would-be entrants. It was inevitable that the curriculum should mirror this and, for some tutors, the movement to 'generic training' in any meaningful sense was difficult. It is hard to recapture this now but the account of Packman (1975) and the novels of John Stroud give some flavour of the powerful commitment and idealism of one group – 'the child care officers', whose rise as an occupational group between 1948 and 1970 was unusually rapid and influential. As some of those social workers became tutors, their interests and professional style in turn affected generations of students. Strong influences were also brought to bear by 'workers turned tutor' from clinical hospital settings. Timms (1964) gives a useful account of developments in psychiatric social work and the training for it and Younghusband (1978, Vol. I, ch. 9) gives a sympathetic description of the position of medical social workers.

An examination of students' reading lists in that period nicely illustrates the dilemma in which educators in the 1950s and early 1960s were caught. There were two strands of social work literature, which did not mesh together easily. The first was one which might be loosely styled 'American generic'. Standard texts were by Biestek (1961), Hollis (1964, 1972) and Perlman (1957). Towle's major work (1954), though largely unread by students, was also powerful in its impact, direct and indirect, on teachers. In fact, the literature epitomises the very considerable American influence on social workers and teachers of the period. Younghusband (1978, Vol. I, p. 83) describes the 'American generosity which enabled British social workers and students to go to the United States for observation and study' and the attachment of American teachers to our institutions. Charlotte Towle herself was consultant to the setting up of the London School of Economics generic course in 1954.

This literature, concentrated upon casework, laid little emphasis upon fields of practice since its concern was to identify generic elements. In any case, these are essentially indigenous: American illustrations meant little to British students. By 1964 one major British contributor, Noel Timms, had gone some way to presenting a 'more local view' but the generic material used by students was none the less heavily weighted by the American authors.

Alongside this there was a British literature, focused upon social work with specific agencies. Each major group had its own journals, which contained some material of high quality and, from 1954, there was *Case Conference*. The 'child care tutors', needing to break new ground in the application of social work to the care of deprived children, quickly collected papers and articles which were universally recommended to students, especially those by Clare Winnicott (1955, 1964). The links between 'agency specific' literature and generic social work were poorly developed, although the work of a few such as Elizabeth Irvine broke new ground. Her seminal article (1952) showed how work in clinical settings could be applied more widely. (Irvine's contribution to generic practice was stimulated by her role as tutor to the Tavistock Clinic Advanced Social Casework Course.) But the very fact that it was on every 'respectable' reading list showed how sparse was such material. Similarly, Hunt's article, first published in 1964, and again, indirectly, a product of 'the Tavistock course', was remarkable at the time for its attempt to show the relevance of social work theory to the probation setting, above all to grasp the nettle of the use of authority, with which so few American writers of the time were concerned, no doubt because most who were qualified worked in voluntary agencies.

In short, therefore, in the twenty years 'before Seebohm',

educators were struggling, as were their colleagues in practice, with complex ideas and emotional attachments, without a solid body of British literature to assist them. It has been suggested in the first chapter that we still have a very long way to go in the development of generic concepts. But we do now have a substantial literature of our own, addressing many different aspects of theory, practice and research. We now have a problem of selecting rather than finding reading for the book list! It was not until the 1970s that British social work educators began to contribute substantially to that literature. (There were a few exceptions but the swallows did not make a summer.)

Whatever the efforts made by the educators to broaden the base of their courses, they were largely doomed to failure whilst the 'professional labels' hung round their students' necks – labels to which cheques for their financial support during training were attached. Knowing the setting in which they were to work, students naturally invested more in particular areas of knowledge and skill. To some extent this remains the same today, notably in relation to probation students, but the separation in earlier times was much more marked, above all, of course, between students heading for different departments of the local authority or for hospitals. The division between graduate and non-graduate entry at one time split 'child care' from 'health and welfare' so that these students did not train together. The fact that hospital social workers had separate employers had a negative, if subtle, effect on 'transferability' whether theoretical or practical. Whatever its difficulties, there seems little doubt that the movement of workers between local authority social services departments and hospitals has been facilitated, both practically and professionally, by the formal change in 1974 whereby social work support for the national health service became the responsibility of the local authority.

Thus at the point that BASW was formed and that the personal social services were about to be reorganised, many social work tutors recognised that generic training was a notion which could only be translated into reality if conditions outside the educational institution were changed.

That there were also educational resistances to change is indisputable. Even today one hears the comment 'It's still really a child care course', and a few courses have managed to retain their specialised identity by a shift to advanced status.

This is not to disparage the contribution made by specialist interests to the education of social workers. Many (of whom I was one) derived lasting benefit from the tightly focused approach of the specialist courses. We have not yet learnt how to preserve the benefits of that and to combine it with a broader education which would inculcate in students greater flexibility, intellectual and emotional. The objective of this necessarily brief review is to show something of the confusion, conflict and tension, and the reasons for it, which characterised social work in the period 1950–70. The end of that period was a landmark in that radical changes, professional, educational and organisational, all took place at about the same time. But the *dramatis personae* did not disappear in a clap of thunder! The cast stayed on stage and on a good many the curtain has yet to fall. There is therefore a continuity which can work both for good and for ill. Reactions to any discussion of specialisation are affected by knowledge, feelings and myths about those twenty years. In particular, the resurgence of discussions about specialisation based upon client groups provokes strong reaction. For some, it is eagerly seized upon as evidence that the old ways were best after all; for others, who were convinced of the need to abandon these groupings as units for service and for training, such trends seem defeatist and retrogressive.

(B) ORGANISATIONAL

The Seebohm Report

It will be clear from the foregoing discussion that the climate was right for organisational change, in the sense that, professionally and educationally, social workers were moving closer together, albeit with some reluctance. This must be linked, however, to wider social and political pressures. The Seebohm Report (1968, p. 19, para 36) points out that a number of important committees had examined aspects of the personal social services between 1948 and 1966 but that none 'was permitted by its terms of reference to examine the organisation of the local authority personal social services as a whole'. They note that most of them 'emphasised the need to improve co-ordination between the local authority services', but that the Ingleby Committee (1960) 'foreshadowed the present enquiry when it said: "it may be that the long term solution will be a re-organisation of the various services concerned with the family and their combination into a unified family service"'.

There were a number of powerful arguments advanced by the Seebohm Committee for this reform, none of which is directly relevant to the theme of this book. For example (pp. 44–8), it considered that a unified service would make it more accessible, that it would attract more resources and that it would facilitate 'intelligence and planning' and hence efficiency. But two key issues which the committee addresses bear directly on specialisation. The first (p. 45), put simply, is that 'the structure of the personal social services ignores the nature of much social distress . . . An integrated social services department will impose few boundaries and require less arbitrary classification of problems.' The second, related point (p. 45) is that: 'because problems are complicated and interdependent, co-ordination . . . is crucial. In many cases, effective help will continue to depend upon the assistance of more than one organisation. But an integrated social services department will ease problems of collaboration.' The committee adds, however, a warning note – that the social services department will have its own problems of co-ordination.

Co-ordination – a key argument

This issue of co-ordination had emerged as of crucial concern in the preceding years. In 1950, an interdepartmental circular had requested local authorities to designate an officer to co-ordinate the activities of those concerned with children in their own homes. The need for local case committees was stressed. The present author, in 1963, published 'Co-ordination reviewed' in which a tentative attempt was made to demonstrate the effects of divided responsibility upon workers' perceptions of family problems. Surprisingly, this modest article, written without benefit of sociological literature, attracted considerable attention and was reprinted in 1967. It would seem, therefore, that it spoke to the conditions of workers in that period. Yet, despite the interest, the Seebohm Report suggested (p. 28) that 'the impression is of very limited success despite the expenditure of much time and energy'.

Careful reading of the Seebohm Report suggests that, as is the fate of most seminal documents, its findings and recommendations have been both simplified and distorted. Certainly, the oft-quoted justification for creating 'one door to knock on', that is, that clients suffered from over-visiting, creates a misleading impression. The numbers of families upon whose door a steady stream of social workers knocked must have been very small. It is salutary and saddening, however, to note that where such problems recur, the reformed structure has done little to reduce them. The probation and education welfare officers remained outside the unified framework, the former being excluded from the committee's terms of reference, their recommendation on the latter being rejected. And it was never envisaged by Seebohm that certain other professionals likely to visit certain families would be incorporated. So the path to the house may still be trodden by, amongst others, health visitors, NSPCC inspectors, housing officials. However large or small the problem of 'multiple visiting' was or is, there is no doubt that major problems of co-ordination and co-operation between workers at field level existed at the time of the committee's deliberations and still do so. The 'post-Seebohm' evidence is striking – in the form of numerous inquiries into the deaths of children, all of which highlight some such failures (Colwell, 1974; Auckland, 1975; Godfrey, 1975; Meurs, 1975; Peacock, 1978). Such difficulties as were exposed in the Maria Colwell inquiry (1974) have been largely untouched by the reorganisation of the personal social services. The major participants – social workers from two authorities, education welfare officers and teachers, school medical officers, health visitors, police and housing officials and the NSPCC were all involved in a network of faulty communication. The best one can say is that without reorganisation there would have been one or two extra professionals involved in such cases – for example, a mental welfare officer and a child care officer representing separate interests.

With hindsight and with the benefit of detailed examination of these cases which have had a tragic outcome, it is clear that, whatever its merits, the reorganisation *per se* did relatively little to promote co-ordination and co-operation even between social workers, leaving aside other professionals and officials with whom social workers in social services departments need to work closely in the interests of the clients. The situation would have been improved had probation officers (as in Scotland) and education welfare officers been brought within social services departments. This is not to say that there would not have been some countervailing disadvantages which it is not the focus of this book to explore. It is simply to emphasise that, although in other ways the implications of the reorganisation have been far-reaching, we have to look elsewhere for the development and fostering of co-ordination and co-operation at field level. The present author, with Christine Hallett, has begun to explore some of these issues in relation to child abuse (Hallett and Stevenson, 1980). But this is only one aspect of a much broader question touching virtually all client groups, especially those for whom health and social care are indivisible. It will be argued later that this may in itself be regarded as grounds for the emergence of new forms of specialisation. It is not the needs of the client alone but the relationship of the network of helpers who may properly be involved that, on occasion, justifies specialist social work input.

Another, more subtle question relevant to the theme of co-ordination concerns the extent to which the unification of training and potentially greater mobility in employment between agencies will offset some of the adverse effects of a narrow definition of agency function. These were amongst the issues explored by the present author before reorganisation (Stevenson, 1963). For example, in two child abuse inquiries (Lisa Godfrey, 1975; Carly Taylor, 1980), the focus

The Issues in Context

of the probation officers upon their adult client seems to have had unfortunate results. It is too soon to say whether this is a transitional problem or whether the impact of the definition of role – including any specialisation which may develop in social services departments – will remain powerful.

Seebohm on specialisation

As Parsloe (1981) remarks, 'the [Seebohm] Report, like the Bible, gives confirmation to strongly held and contradictory viewpoints'. Certainly, it has been used both to confirm and to refute the notion of generic social workers, as distinct from generic teams. In view of these doubts, it is worth examining the committee's statements on this point in some detail. (They are to be found in Part V, Chapter XVII of the report.)

First, the evidence given to the committee on specialisation is considered. It is interesting that 'much was said on training but relatively little on specialisation', but that one of the most outspoken critics of the existing arrangements was the British Medical Association, which referred (p. 159) to 'confusion on both the part of the general practitioner and the public', and to 'too high a degree of specialisation early on in the social worker's career with consequent isolation of groups of social workers according to departmental aims'. Nevertheless, the committee comments (p. 159) that although the evidence 'was generally in favour of changes in the present pattern of specialisation, with only a few exceptions those submitting evidence either envisaged patterns essentially similar to those existing at present or did not go into details on what new pattern they thought should evolve'. This politely phrased observation perhaps masks a fundamental problem which, unresolved, has bedevilled the development of social services departments in the past decade. Bluntly, the professionals had not done enough homework to produce plans or models of service delivery for the committee to consider and with which the new social services departments could experiment. The profession did not like what it had got but had very little idea of what it wanted. Even as influential and as thoughtful a group as the Association of Psychiatric Social Workers thought it likely that 'three main areas of specialisation would remain: in physical illness and disability, including old age; in overt mental disorder; and in "general family problems"'. (Note the absence of mental handicap.)

This unpreparedness might not have mattered so much if the creation of new social services departments had not been accompanied by other massive distractions from the fundamental task which they faced, that of creating new structures to serve clients better. As Parsloe (1981) has shown, the area team sprang into being with surprisingly little discussion of its purposes, scope and focus, and a central facet of its functioning, that of specialisation, was allowed to grow like Topsy in most authorities. Soon afterwards, as is well known, most social services departments were caught up in another tide of local government reorganisation. They battled with the increase in demand consequent in part upon new legislation for which they were under-resourced, such as the Chronically Sick and Disabled Persons Act 1970; in part upon predictable demographic trends, mainly an increase in the numbers of frail elderly people; and in part upon unpredictable social trends such as the increased public concern about, and awareness of, non-accidental injury to children. All this took place against a background of a field service only partly professionally qualified and stated government policies of community care which increased the expectations of social work support. From 1974 onwards the wave of child abuse inquiries stirred public and professional anxiety and this in turn affected the development of staff and hence, indirectly, trends in specialisation. The reorganisation of the health service in 1974 further affected the role of social services departments in the provision of social work service.

The effect of these familiar and well-documented stresses accounts, at least in part, for the failure of social services departments systematically to evolve and monitor patterns of specialisation which are crucial to the well-being of clients, and to the perceived effectiveness of social work by other professionals. We cannot know whether the story would have been different, despite the subsequent stresses, if social workers, in practice and in education, had been clearer conceptually and more positive in their suggestions at an earlier stage (even if they had been proved wrong).

The Seebohm Committee (pp. 159–60) made an attempt to group the different elements which were put forward as justifying specialisation. It outlined three: first, 'administrative reasons', such as 'the need for the worker to be available at unusual hours; the need to be able to concentrate on a particular field of difficult and time-consuming work . . . and the need to limit the points of contact with which other services have to deal'. Secondly, there were 'reasons bound up with the temperament and inclination of individual workers' and, thirdly, *the professional arguments, the view that some kinds of social work demand a higher concentration of interest, a detailed knowledge and a particular attitude of mind*' (my italics).

As will be shown in later chapters, these groupings are not satisfactory. For example, the reasons subsumed under 'administrative' merge into important professional and interprofessional considerations and overlap with matters of personal temperament and preference. That the committee was not persuaded by the third group of 'professional arguments' may be indicated by the fact that they were not illustrated or discussed in the report. This makes it difficult to know how much weight could reasonably have been attached to them. They occupy only half a page of the report and the committee passes on quickly to 'the case for a new approach', having commented (p. 160): 'We see the force in these arguments and we recognise that there will be strict statutory requirements which the social services departments must meet.' (This reference to 'statutory work' does not follow clearly from the previous arguments for specialisation and is not developed.) 'Nevertheless,' it continues, 'subject to certain important provisos . . . we consider that a family or individual in need of social care, should, as far as is possible, be served by a single social worker . . . The new department, by escaping from the rigid classifications implied in the present symptom centred approach, will provide a more effective family service.'

This statement, as it stands, does not make the case for a generic social worker, in the sense of one who carries a mixed caseload of different client groups. It would be perfectly possible for a single worker to take only selected cases from which certain groups or problems were excluded. The emphasis here is only that the client should not receive a fragmented service. Though not described as such, a 'key worker' is clearly envisaged (p. 160, para. 517). However, in what follows it seems that the committee was hoping that social workers would avoid the 'narrow specialisation' which would have 'a detrimental effect on professional judgement'. It gives as an example (p. 160) that specialised work with 'grossly disturbed and socially inadequate families can adversely influence the assessment which workers make of the level at which such families can function'. This is an odd example to use given its concern that service should not be fragmented, for these are the families where over-visiting is a real possibility. It is also a good illustration of an argument adduced without the countervailing points to balance it, which is apparent in this part of the committee's report. Before it is accepted and it is decided to abolish Family Service Units, NSPCC Special Units, or their equivalent in social services departments, one has at least to examine the merits of such specialisation and how its disadvantages might be overcome.

Some of the merits relate to the points which the committee had put to it – concentration of effort, personal inclination and particular professional skills. The points are exceptionally well illustrated by Mattinson and Sinclair (1980) in their study of intensive marital work with a group of highly disturbed clients in the social services department of a busy London borough. Some of the disadvantages for workers may be overcome by ensuring a varied experience over time, from training through practice. The narrowness which the committee rightly feared is not an inevitable consequence of a period of planned specialisation.

The committee acknowledges that there may be occasions when it is necessary and appropriate to involve more than one social worker. It cites as examples problems involving adolescence or marriage. Again, one need not necessarily infer from that that the 'key worker' should have a caseload spanning all types of client and problem. Perhaps the clearest statement of the committee's views is the following (p. 161):

> On first entry to the service, the range of work of the newly qualified worker would normally be limited. However, he would be expected as soon as possible to undertake a wider range of social work functions and to develop skill in them. He might develop interests in particular aspects of the work of the department and it would be right for him to be enabled to pursue such *concentrations of interest, always provided that this did not conflict with the primary objective of giving people the help they needed at the right time.* (My italics)

There are a number of interesting points embedded in this paragraph. First, it is assumed that there is a progression towards genericism; secondly, the phrase 'concentrations of interest' is presumably chosen to avoid the term 'specialisation' and the distinction here appears to be between informal and formal developments. Thirdly, the proviso in italics implies that specialisation might work against the immediate interests of clients. This might be so: if, for example, a worker's intense informal interest in work with adolescents made him unwilling or incompetent to take on an elderly person urgently needing help. But, equally, a degree of specialisation, especially if it is formally designated, may in fact ensure that a client who would otherwise 'go to the bottom of the pile' *does* receive 'the help he needs at the right time'.

The remainder of the chapter serves further to confuse 'the message' of the report on specialisation, if such message there be. Attachment to institutions (such as schools, health centres, or courts) is briefly discussed and it is envisaged (p. 161) that:

> eventually a worker would be *attached* [original italics] on a *fairly* [my italics] long term basis, although he would be based on and keep close to the social services department. These workers would be primarily concerned with problems arising within the institutions ... but would not be specialised in the present sense, because ... they would be concerned with the whole family and not only with a member attending the institution and would follow through, dealing with problems which were not directly connected with the institution.

There are professional and administrative problems in this point which will be further examined in succeeding chapters. Suffice it to say here that the time needed to create and to sustain effective interprofessional links of this kind may make it difficult for the worker to take on substantial areas of work unconnected with the agency to which he is attached. But much depends on the history and circumstances of a particular agency and on their varying size and demands.

The committee refers (p. 162) to the need for specialisation above field level, 'not least to help in the advancement of knowledge'. It hopes that 'as the service develops, specialisations will cluster differently and new types . . . emerge to meet new problems and needs and fresh conceptions of how these might be tackled'. Apparently this is envisaged at team level as well as at 'headquarters', since the committee, whilst stating that 'it would be unwise to attempt to define these needs', specifically mentions the need for specialisation at both levels in relation to residential care and community work.

Finally, it reaffirms (p. 162) that the new departments will only work well if 'a serious effort is made to break down divisions from the beginning'.

What, therefore, emerges from this scrutiny is that there was a conspicuous lack of clarity as to what was intended regarding specialisation. The issues were (and are) extremely complex and, as has been suggested, the committee was not much helped by the evidence of professional groups. What is clear is the following:

that it wished divisions of caseloads by the existing client groups to disappear;

that it was most anxious to avoid overlapping service to individual clients and families;

that it did not rule out some informal specialisation at field level, though it was not put forward with enthusiasm;

that it saw a need for some formal specialisation at senior levels, though the arguments for it were not well developed;

that it had little idea of different ways in which the cake might be cut as new 'clusters' of specialisation grew.

The Act, passed in 1970, was implemented in April 1971. Local authorities had little time to plan after its enactment, although those with more foresight might perhaps have seen the direction in which the wind was blowing for some years and begun to plan accordingly. Unfortunately, what the new social services departments actually did was not systematically monitored nationally. One study of 'Seatown' (Goldberg and Warburton, 1979) took a snapshot in 1972 and again in 1975. It was found (p. 12) that in the early days caseloads were 'still highly specialised and most thought that specialisation would continue indefinitely and considered this to be desirable'. By 1975 caseloads were more mixed, though (p. 15) 'a considerable number expressed reservations about the generic social worker'. Our research, which was in effect a snapshot of thirty-one area teams in the period between 1976 and 1977, showed that most accepted the idea of a basic grade social worker's competence to handle a range of client problems and did not argue against generic training. However, the composition of caseloads showed a considerable degree of informal specialisation, first, in the concentration upon children and families – a point also noted in the 1972 Goldberg and Warburton survey, that is, before the inquiries into the deaths of children gained momentum. Secondly, the extent of the dominant interest in this area of work was shown by informal specialisation *within* that client grouping, for example, in work with adolescents, intermediate treatment, and so on, whilst it was conspicuously lacking in other client groups.

It is apparent both from the Seebohm Report and from the research referred to above that the terms 'generic' and 'specialised' were in Britain used almost exclusively in relation to the focus of individual workers on client groupings or problems, rather than to modes of intervention or to organisational arrangements. In an attempt both to clarify and to expand the implications of the term 'specialisation', the present author (with Hallett and Strachan) described the structures and modes of specialisation found in the area teams studied, even although the term was not always used by our respondents to describe them. Chapter VII of the report, briefly summarised here, suggests four ways of considering specialisation and their relevance to the teams we studied.

(i) *Informal specialisation*

This refers to the special interests of workers. It may be in relation to client groups, methods of social work, or certain projects or tasks assigned to team members. In our study the first of these was by far the most common and, within it, sub-groupings of children and families, for example, work with adolescents or one-parent families. There was little 'method' specialisation but rather more 'by task or project', for example, liaison with clubs and day centres and intermediate treatment.

(ii) *Formal specialisation at practitioner level*

Not all such specialists are social workers. For example, we found a number of occupational therapists, though not always based within teams. There was considerable variation in the extent to which occupational therapists undertook what might be described as social work tasks for the handicapped, and the division of roles between social workers and occupational therapists was unclear.

There were eight community workers attached to teams – raising the question as to whether they are defined as social workers. Otherwise, formal specialisms either within teams or serving them were almost exclusively for work with the visually handicapped or the deaf – and there were not many of these, five workers with the visually handicapped and three with the deaf.

(iii) *Specialisation in the organisation of work*

Most of this centred upon arrangements for duty and intake work.

(iv) *Specialist advisers outside the team*

The picture here – reflecting, however, only the perspective of the team – was that there was widespread dissatisfaction and uncertainty as to what such advisers could and should offer to the teams in terms of advice and support, and whether they were management advisers at a higher level in the hierarchy or specialists with executive functions who had more narrowly defined tasks, for example, 'intermediate treatment officer'.

The next two chapters take up these and other ways of looking at specialisation. Our research revealed relatively few attempts to innovate and experiment. It was almost as if people did not know how to begin. The discussion which follows is intended to stimulate a debate in what is probably one of the most complex areas of policy in service delivery.

CHAPTER 3

The Notion of Expertise

Any discussion under this heading cannot duck the ambiguity and confusion surrounding attempts to delineate the social work task. For the first question – 'expertise in what?' – raises the issues which have been debated exhaustively and exhaustingly for at least thirty years, though with mounting intensity and a somewhat different emphasis in the last decade. It is inevitable that a view of desirable expertise is determined by one's assumptions concerning the nature of social work, both as it is and as it ought to be. For workers in social services departments, there seem to be two key issues which are recurring themes throughout this book.

First, the very idea of expertise causes some people's hackles to rise. The term quickly slides into 'elitism' and is sometimes associated with negative elements in professionalism. This is an attitude with which I have no sympathy. When we as citizens are in difficulty we hope, and have a right to expect, that those who are paid to help us will have some expertise that we do not possess. We are irritated by those who cannot address themselves effectively to our problems. The clients of social workers are entitled to expert help, as are the clients of doctors and electricians.

The confusion in this approach stems in part from lack of self-confidence, but those who espouse what Parsloe (1981) has described as 'a community ideology' compound it by the argument that 'the oppressed client' must be given 'access to knowledge he did not have and hence to increased power'. Thus, 'social workers . . . share their knowledge and diminish their power'. However desirable this may be in the long run, it does not absolve the social worker from the responsibility of having some knowledge to share.

Secondly, and much more cogently, there is the question

of what kind of expertise is required. Here one must distinguish between how things are and how one may think they ought to be. It is well known that a great deal of social work time in social services departments is presently taken up with what is described as 'advice, advocacy and brokerage'. This does not of itself delineate an area of expertise which it is essential for social workers to acquire. It could equally be argued that these activities should be performed by others – a point to which I shall return. However that may be resolved, there remains an inescapable tension concerning the areas of expertise which are considered to be relevant. Clearly this is influenced by one's explanations of the causes of social dysfunctioning. Explanations, however, do not necessarily *determine* 'treatment' and therefore do not determine desired expertise. A doctor may treat with drugs whilst believing that his patient's dis-ease is caused by social or psychological factors which he feels powerless to treat. Social workers may accept, as many do, that the root causes of many family problems lie in wider social conditions and yet seek to alleviate stress by family-focused work. None the less, what is perceived to be most important will crucially affect the knowledge and skill the worker seeks to acquire. In social services departments today two strands can be seen. First, there is the distinction between individual and community models of pathology which may lead the social worker in different directions in the search for expertise. Secondly, there is conflict between the value of what might crudely be described as 'book learning' or 'person learning'. Devaluation of knowledge acquired indirectly through the work of others is common in social work. But it is perhaps especially evident in those whose community ideology leads them towards a search for expertise derived from intimate knowledge of certain localities. Intrinsic to their stance is the idea that knowledge is not 'out there' but inside the groups and communities with which they are working.

With this acknowledgement of the problems which 'the notion of expertise' raises for social workers and which require further examination, it is helpful none the less to put the matter in a wider perspective.

Specialisation in work is universal in advanced societies and has attracted sociological comment from Durkheim onwards. There are two forms of specialisation. The first is concerned with the need for special expertise to provide service, which is the subject of this chapter. The second concerns the division of work for greater efficiency. This is discussed in the next chapter. Although the two forms overlap to a considerable extent in social work organisations, they are conceptually distinct.

Specialisation within professions

Much of the relevant sociological literature deals with the rise of the professions generally. Here we are looking at the emergence of sub-specialisms. The conventional case for this is that certain tasks are performed better, to the benefit of the client, patient, or consumer by someone who has narrowed the scope of his work and thus has the opportunity to learn more in depth and detail about certain aspects of it. Bucher and Strauss (1961) are amongst the few sociologists who examine the processes involved. They refer to 'the segments' within professions and the different aspirations, values and conflicts which underlie their development. It is important to acknowledge that in social work, as in other professions, there are complex forces, organisational and professional, which will influence, if not determine, the emergence of these 'segments' and that it would be naive to claim that client interest is the sole determinant. Indeed, the earlier discussion of the struggle to move towards unification illustrates this point.

Analogies can readily be made between social work and other professions of which 'segments' are characteristic. It should be noted, however, that they now rest upon a generic base – medical and legal, for example – exemplified by educational systems which lead to accreditation.

The most common reason advanced to justify the emergence of such specialisation within social work and, indeed, in other professions, is that the sheer volume of knowledge and range of skill required to cope adequately with the tasks encompassed by the profession is too great unless sub-divided. Reference is usually made to the 'knowledge explosion'. There is undoubtedly force in this argument, given the advances in the natural social sciences upon which most professions, including social work, draw. To take but one topical example: empirical research into the factors associated with child abuse has mushroomed in the last fifteen years. (There were 700 papers presented to the 1978 International Congress on Child Abuse.) Unquestionably, those who work in this field need to be acquainted with the current thinking if their practice is to be of an acceptable standard.

The model of a professional specialist, however, merits further examination. A teacher may specialise in 'a subject' or in a category of child; a lawyer in an aspect of the law or in a type of activity, such as advocacy, or both; a doctor in an aspect of medicine based upon bodily systems but sometimes involving the exercise of certain technical skills as in surgery. They differ therefore in the rationale for specialisation. It is not until we ask – what is the purpose of the professional exchange? – that the justification, or lack of it, for specialisation emerges. For a person wanting advice on contract law, there is less benefit to be derived from being served by an expert on, say, criminal law. The problem and therefore the need may be categorised in the terms in which the law is categorised and the fit is comfortable enough. The medical profession, however, cannot always claim such a comfortable fit. Whilst it is undoubtedly true that expertise in the workings of sub-systems of the body is required, there are dangers to some patients if this fragmentation of knowledge is not accompanied by some attempt at integration. Those countries which have not had an equivalent to the British general practitioner have been made uncomfortably aware of this. The teacher also faces problems: subject expertise, without expertise in teaching, based upon an understanding of an individual child, will carry the teacher some way but not far enough. And the younger or the more unusual the child, the more necessary this understanding becomes. Thus specialisation in teaching may be subject-centred or child-centred, and this creates tension, often affecting status within the profession. Many other examples could be given.

Furthermore, the case for specialist expertise and for the forms it takes is only in part made by reference to particular areas of knowledge and skill. It reflects the priorities of the professions and these are not always congruent with the welfare of the consumers of the services, actual or potential. Thus, the specialism of medical geriatrics has been slow to develop and to attract prestige. Arguments against it have been advanced, although it would seem hard to deny that there are certain medical problems particularly associated with ageing which justify specialist advice and treatment. It may be that the reluctance to admit 'geriatrics' to the range of specialisms is indicative of a wider problem, the pessimism and devaluation which surround old age in our society.

Similarly, in social work, it cannot be assumed that emergent specialisms mirror client need. As in any other profession, various factors will influence their development. These will include the values and priorities accorded to certain clients and problems both in society generally and in the agency (which is affected, *inter alia*, by statute), and pressure from other professions. Individual interest also plays a part but formal specialisation grows more from extrinsic factors. Most people choose what is available; there are only a few 'trail-blazers'.

Recent interest in the application of systems theory and integrated methods to social work highlights some of the dilemmas involved in, and opportunities for, the definition and development of specialism. As was discussed in Chapter 1 there is a sense in which the generalist becomes a specialist. There are parallels with other professions. Most medical specialisms relate to sub-systems of the body; but they are, of course, inter-related, and treatment of one may have effects upon another. Similarly, the teacher ignores at his peril the interaction of intellectual, emotional and social components in his pupil's learning. Exactly the same problem confronts social work. No compelling logic leads one to formal specialisation on the basis of a particular client group or method of intervention, when one considers the individual family or wider community as interacting systems and the mode of intervention is determined by reference to the 'target for change'.

A characteristic of the specialisms in other professions referred to earlier is that the model is one of direct interaction between specialist and consumer (or patient). There is, for example, no formal arrangement whereby medical specialists advise general practitioners about a case without seeing the patient concerned – though no doubt this happens on occasion. (Whether this should be formalised is an interesting question.) The position in social work merits close examination. Our research indicates that social services departments have not found a way to utilise profitably the knowledge and experience of certain specialist advisers, who do not usually have direct contact with the clients.[1] The fieldworkers interviewed in our project placed little value upon their contribution and were, indeed, very uncertain as to 'what they did'. There were various organisational reasons for this, but there were also disturbing implications of the lack of value placed upon specialist knowledge and skill in social service organisations. The most cursory examination of the problems with which social services departments deal reveals the wide range of knowledge which is required. Not all of this, of course, is necessarily or properly within the domain of social work. But a great deal *is* necessary for the social work task to be adequately performed and, as yet, the possession of such knowledge has been ascribed little formal value within the organisation.

The crucial question, therefore, to be addressed is, in my view, not whether there should be formally designated 'experts' within social services departments – this we should surely take for granted – but what their specialism should be, what their role should be and how they should relate to the structure as a whole.

How should specialist expertise be fostered and utilised?
Rowbottom *et al.* (1974) give some consideration to these issues. They discuss the role of consultants and, having acknowledged the need for informal advice-giving between colleagues, they continue (pp. 125–6): 'the department might well recognise the need to bring to bear high level

specialist advice more generally throughout its work'. They ask: 'Would those who fill such a role really act in a purely consultant, i.e. advisory capacity? Could the advice always be freely taken or freely left? . . . If a department has workers of such specialist knowledge is it not likely to need to harness their skills more systematically than in merely providing a resource to be used at will in individual case work?'

They suggest two distinct roles, those of *specialist practitioners* and *specialist co-ordinators*. The former, who would carry cases, might advise or work directly. The latter 'would be responsible for promoting developments generally'. The word 'co-ordination' is used to indicate that they would not carry managerial authority. (The term, however, does less than justice to the tasks they wish to ascribe to such a role.) They conclude (p. 127): 'Clearly the two roles might be combined . . . junior specialists might have a larger proportion of specialist "practitioner" than "co-ordinator" work and vice versa.'

What is proposed here bears some resemblance to this, except that it would seem unprofitable to pursue the development of relatively senior specialist co-ordinator posts as such until more successful ways have been found of specifying their function within the organisation as a whole. Otherwise they may look remarkably like the ill-starred specialist advisers.

So far as specialist practitioners are concerned, it is possible (and tempting) to devise alternatives to the conventional client groupings, but it may be unprofitable to swim against a tide. For such knowledge is 'packaged' not only for social workers but for others in the helping professions around certain typologies – 'handicap', 'child abuse', 'delinquency', for example. This carries some dangers for division of work, which are examined in the next chapter. But it makes good sense for the organisation to give to certain individuals the responsibility for acquiring and disseminating relevant knowledge and skill, and it is likely that it will be easier to do this if the more conventional groupings are accepted, provided attempts are made to link them each to the other.

The model with which it seems most profitable to experiment takes into account recent trends, albeit tentative, in 'career grade' social work and should be dependent upon the acceptance by employers of the need for post-qualifying education. It is depressing that such developments are certain to be seriously held back by the present economic and social climate. But to ignore this pressing need for further education in social work is fundamentally to endanger the quality of service offered. Let us take, as an example, the topic of most current concern, that of child abuse. Reference was made earlier to the 'knowledge explosion' in that area, in which a number of professions have joint concern. Professional competence demands that social workers should be aware of the implications of recent important research for the assessment and treatment of families and be able to make some appraisal of its reliability. That is but one example of many but it is particularly vivid and sadly topical in its 'life and death' implications. Knowledge never removes the need for judgement; predictors are never absolute. But without knowledge, judgement is not informed

As Malherbe (1979, p. 64) points out, if, as many think it should, social work in this country moves towards accreditation, 'their accountability in law is likely to be increased – and it may be necessary to reach agreement on a definition of norms of adequate professional care and conduct'. One of the three criteria on which social workers may be judged in court in a civil action for negligence is 'the acceptable degree of professional learning, skill and ability' judged by the standards of the profession as a whole.

Without wishing to increase the already high levels of anxiety which exist in social workers at the present time, this point serves to emphasise the importance of explicit acknowledgement of the need for expertise.

It does not follow, however, that such knowledge needs always to be located in the person dealing with the case. But there are problems if the people given this responsibility are, or are believed to be, removed too far from the 'action'. The idea of career grade social workers who specialise in direct work with certain groups, but whose responsibility is also to share with their colleagues their particular knowledge, has attractions. It is possible to envisage a number of named experts, in fields defined as crucial by the agency, who would act as consultants and contribute to in-service training throughout the organisation. This already happens to an extent within teams and sometimes (though rarely) between them. But what is suggested here is a planned, systematic development of key specialists, available to everyone as a resource, and with some role in direct service which provides ongoing experience and credibility. There is no need for such social workers to be at a very senior level; indeed, it might be the natural first step for many who have gained general experience and want to deepen their knowledge and skill in a particular area. To use experienced colleagues for advice and support is congenial to social workers, who dislike the bureaucratic model of hierarchical authority. There would be problems of accountability between such a person in that role and the team leader or his equivalent. Surely, however, these are not insuperable?

Our interviews with social services team members showed that many who had 'biased caseloads' were used informally by colleagues for advice. What is proposed is not a substitute for such exchanges but these informal arrangements alone are not adequate. The agency has formally to ascribe value to such specialisation, for without it opportunities for further education will not be fostered and the person will not be legitimated in the role within the agency as a whole, or whatever segment of it is appropriate. There are powerful forces working against such developments in the relative insularity of many teams. Thus it is possible for lights to be hidden under bushels and the resources of the department to be inadequately utilised.

There can be no blueprint for such planned specialisation, for local needs and conditions vary greatly. But an analysis of these needs and conditions may provide the rationale for a coherent strategy, and provide a valuable check to collusion with social or political pressures which may encourage *ad hoc* developments with no overall plan.

The dangers of formal specialisation

Thus far the discussion has centred upon the need for specialist expertise, of both knowledge and skill, to be developed within social services departments and to be made generally available. The longer-term consequences of increased specialisation in practice, however, have been little debated in the social work literature. There are dangers well recognised in organisational sociology. Moore (1964, p. 53) draws attention to this. In discussing factors involved in social change in group structure, he points to the variables 'that are predicted to be negatively correlated with individual impact on organisations'. These include 'rigidity and specificity of nominal role requirements, specialisation of position and roles'.

Presthus (1979, p. 21) points to the 'inherent tension between those in hierarchical positions of authority and those who play specialised roles'. He points out that

> those in hierarchical positions often find the specialists difficult. Rarely can they be persuaded that their own department does not deserve the lion's share of the organisation's resources . . . The conflict is often one between the organisation's view of the administrator and the restricted perspective of the specialist. Moreover, specialists disturb the equilibrium of the organisation by fighting amongst themselves about resources and recognition . . . specialisation can become pathological . . .

Whilst this powerful critique may somewhat overstate the problem for social services departments, any suggestions for formal specialisation carry with them a certain inevitable 'nuisance value'; they will, to an extent, disrupt the organisation. The balance between the healthy and stimulating conflict of competing demands and fighting blindly for one's corner is hard to keep. Certainly, specialisation reduces organisational mobility; even the encouragement of informal interests in staff creates a potential problem of service deficiency when a worker moves, in that, for example, a particular form of treatment, such as group-work, may be offered by a team member only to be withdrawn when that member leaves and there is no one else to fill the gap. But the issue is more complex and far-reaching that that. Specialisation, as was seen in 'pre-Seebohm' days, frequently encourages us to put on professional and organisational blinkers. Whilst we all have to put boundaries around the work we must do, those who manage organisations have to watch that those boundaries are not so narrow or so rigid as to do a disservice to clients, as the Seebohm Committee (1968) recognised. This can take the form of a direct disservice to individuals or families, as when a worker sees only the problem of the adolescent and does not relate it to that of the grandmother who is living with the family. Equally important, it can be an indirect disservice in that the knowledge and skill available in one aspect of the work is not utilised in relation to another, as when studies of the dynamics of family violence in relation to child abuse are not utilised in cases of 'battered wives'. Furthermore, once a specialism has been created, there is a human tendency for it to become 'a protected area', whose perpetuation is defended.

The Seebohm Committee (1968) sought through reorganisation to minimise these tendencies. Ten years later we have to re-examine organisation and practice, to see how far we can reconcile a proven need for new forms of specialisation with a flexible response to clients' diverse needs. We have also to take into account a new factor, the rise of the Certificate in Social Service training with its highly specialised structure and the impact this will make on social services departments as the numbers of those thus qualified grow. This will be considered further in the last chapter.

I have argued for the development of some formal specialisation by experienced practitioners. Whilst this suggestion carries with it the risk of rigidity in staff deployment, the level at which the specialisation is developed within the agency may help to counteract this tendency. Used as a stepping stone for some, such posts would be re-examined as they became vacant. The organisation of the team as a whole, discussed in the next chapter, is another crucial factor. The need for responsive and flexible deployment of staff, whilst always important, is particularly crucial at a stage in social work when the scope and limitations of the task are still unclear. There is a tension between, on the one hand, the danger of premature crystallisation of organisational roles which inhibits innovation and, on the other, a fluidity which reflects uncertainty and confusion. The latter may result in a proliferation of informal, unacknowledged specialisms and reactive rather than innovative behaviour, either because of external pressures or because certain forms of specialisation become fashionable.

In summary: this chapter has discussed the need for expertise in social work which suggests a need to specialise; it has drawn parallels with other professions and has argued that such specialisms are essential for competent service, although the nature of the expertise required will continue to be the subject of debate. It is acknowledged that such developments carry with them dangers of new rigidities in the structure of departments and that the level, qualifications and role of such specialists will need careful planning and monitoring.

NOTE: CHAPTER 3

1 Further research, funded by the Research Liaison Group for the Physically Disabled (DHSS), on this issue is being carried out at the University of Keele.

Chapter 4

The Organisation of Work (I)

(A) THE PATCH SYSTEM

Thus far specialisation has been considered in terms of individual workers possessing, or being encouraged to develop, expertise which is made available to the team or, in some cases, to the department more generally. We turn now to the other key issue, the organisation of work.

Skill through experience

Although in social work these two elements in specialisation interact, they are conceptually different. Specialisation may exist on the factory floor: traditionally, for example, there has been a high degree of division of labour on the conveyor belt, it being apparent that efficiency is thus increased. Whilst it is possible that, in repeating one action the actor becomes more proficient or 'expert', this is not the same kind of expertise as that claimed, for example, by the professional paediatrician or the primary school teacher. The 'conveyor belt' comparison should not be ignored, however, for it highlights two important points. First, many social workers who at present would not claim expertise in the professional sense would admit that sheer familiarity with a certain range of tasks brings greater proficiency. This 'practice wisdom' is not to be underestimated. It raises one of the problems which confront students, educators and newly qualified generic workers.

Whatever arguments are advanced in favour of a generic educational base and whatever progress is made in the formulation of bridging concepts, there are facets to particular areas of social work which are learnt by the repeated application of theory to particular cases which have certain elements in common or by, quite simply, the repetition of experience. The present author attempted to show this in a case example of a short-stay reception of children into care (Stevenson, 1978). That there are theoretical elements relevant not only to such receptions but also to other comparable situations (such as the admission of elderly persons to a home on holiday) does not alter the fact that the worker learns to take into account particular matters which bear upon the management of the case. These may be related to the age of the children, the employment of the father which affects visiting arrangements, the preparation of the foster parents, and so on. After a while the worker experienced in child welfare should become more skilful in carrying out the task, anticipating certain problems and likely solutions. The task becomes less stressful for the worker since repetition increases familiarity and thereby reduces anxiety. (Confidence in performance is not, however, to be confused with desensitisation of workers to the trauma for the individual concerned.)

A crucial matter for decision, therefore, is whether the needs of certain client groups are so particular and encountered so rarely that a generalist worker simply will not gain the experience to deal with them adequately. An example, perhaps the most obvious in present social services clientele, is that of the mentally handicapped and their relatives. The numbers are small relative to other groups, such as the elderly, and it is possible that a generalist social worker will have very few of such cases at any one time. Browne (1979) has shown in some detail how complicated are some of the developmental tasks which confront parents of mentally handicapped children. Whilst it is not necessarily the social worker's task to advise on specific aspects of child-rearing, for this may more properly fall to the health visitor or psychologist, the social worker needs to be sufficiently conversant with such cases to be able to distinguish between the common and the uncommon problem and to reassure or to suggest referral. It is very unlikely that a newly qualified social worker will have derived that requisite knowledge from a basic course.

If effective help to such clients is to be offered there are two ways open to the agency. One is to encourage specialisation; the other is to look to the supervisor. The present situation in social services departments dooms the latter course to defeat. For it is common ground that the priorities accorded to certain client groups, linked to the continuing shortage of qualified workers, means that many supervisors will not themselves have had the relevant experience with certain clients or problems and will therefore be unlikely to bring to supervision the same rigour and precision in respect of all the cases which are ostensibly their responsibility. However, were the idea of 'career grade specialists' to be developed, it would be feasible to involve the appropriate person in consultation or review. Thus this problem in itself is not a sufficient argument for task specialisation. Moreover, returning to the earlier analogy of the factory floor, it is well known that on the car assembly lines some of the apparent merits of highly specialised activity are offset (and reflected in lower productivity) by boredom. Whilst at first sight this might seem irrelevant to the complex tasks performed by social workers, our research suggested that many social workers derived enjoyment from the wide range of activities which they undertook. This cannot be lightly cast aside.

A further point sometimes advanced in favour of task specialisation concerns not simply the efficiency born of carrying through more frequently the same activity, but the confidence which comes from having to confront and cope with feelings about particular client groups – feelings of fear about adolescents, perhaps, or of aesthetic revulsion at gross physical disability. Here again the wide spread of people and problems which the social worker faces makes it likely that there will be particular groups with whom he feels less comfortable, with whose difficulties he cannot readily empathise, sometimes because of the unconscious or suppressed reactions they call out in him. There is a strong case for seeking to ensure that all social work students have an opportunity to face their reactions to a range of 'likely problems' but, realistically, it is quite possible that a student will end his course without having had such opportunities across the board. In itself, this cannot be a valid reason for specialisation. That decision will be more soundly made, however, if the initial fears or anxieties have been exposed and to some extent overcome in the early stages of a professional career.

So far, examples of 'task division' have been drawn from the conventional client groupings and the discussion has centred upon the likely effect on client service and job satisfaction of formal specialisation by individuals. These groupings are, however, but one of many possible ways of 'cutting the cake'. We need to consider alternative models of task division which may make the service more effective. The criteria relevant to this have first to be identified; they are not mutually exclusive. *It is the weight ascribed to them which will determine the extent and form of specialisation.*

The factors which determine specialisation

There are five factors which have to be balanced, the one against the other, in addition to that of specialist expertise, discussed above. These are:

first, the value ascribed to service by the same individual(s) to a given geographical area;

secondly, the value ascribed to communication, co-operation and collaboration between social workers and other workers actually or potentially involved with the same clients (this may take the form of service from a team, with or without attachment or liaison arrangements, or it may be offered within a host organisation);

thirdly, the arrangements made for work to be organised more efficiently to the benefit of clients ('intake' is the common example but there are many other possible variations);

fourthly, the needs perceived by social services departments for specialisms, either because of the unusual skills required (social work with the deaf, for example), or because of the need to develop certain skills and/or resources (finding foster and adoptive homes, for example);

fifthly, allowance for individual staff members to develop special interests, which may not be formally described as specialisms but which have implications for the allocation of work.

Another factor to be noted is the practice of allocating certain tasks deemed to be more complex or carrying a high degree of risk to the qualified and most experienced members of staff. This may create *de facto* specialism in which, for example, all cases involving children at risk are carried by certain persons. Obviously the effect of this is variable between departments, depending on the ratio of qualified staff to the total complement and on the criteria for the award of the new salary levels, agreed with the National Joint Committee. Whilst recognising this situation as a fact of life, it is only desirable as an aspect of planned specialisation if it reflects a clear policy, founded on professional assessment, that certain work can and should be done by the more qualified and experienced; that is to say, it is a desired arrangement and does not simply arise *faute de mieux*.

Geographical divisions and the patch system
Obviously all social service delivery has to be divided according to geographical boundaries: the structure of local government imposes the outer boundary but, within that, there will be sub-divisions. The emphasis placed upon such arrangements, however, varies considerably. It may simply reflect a preoccupation of employers with travelling expenses (a constraint which, however mundane, has to be taken into account). But some social workers are committed to the idea of 'knowing their patch' and see this as carrying advantages which outweigh those of the specialisation which is possible when such boundaries are less significant in the allocation of work. As we pointed out in our research report (p. 169) there are apparent 'common sense' differences between urban and rural areas, the former seeming to offer more opportunities for specialisation than the latter, in which the area to be covered is so much larger. Within an area served by a team, however, further sub-divisions are possible and practice varied greatly, even in rural areas. Some adhered quite rigidly to allocation of work to a patch worker. Others permitted alternative arrangements for various reasons, including the bringing in of a worker with special expertise from another

area for that case. One rural area, in Wales, rejected a patch system altogether. 'This was an experienced and qualified team of social workers . . . they had their own special interests and several clearly felt more "comfortable" with certain client groups than others' (p. 65). Similarly, in a field study completed after the others and not included in the report, social workers in a remote area of Scotland operated a 'specialist service' despite travelling distances.

Thus it appears, not for the first time, that one man's 'common sense' is not another's and that there are underlying assumptions and values which affect these seemingly practical arrangements. One of the most important concerns the definition of, and importance ascribed to, 'knowing the community'. A respondent (p. 65) remarked: 'It has given me a great deal of confidence. I know my way around and can get the feel of the area. I feel out on a limb if I go elsewhere.' The question is, however, whether this confidence enables a better service to be rendered to the clients. As Halsey (in Bulmer, 1978, p. 149) points out: '[The word community] has so many meanings as to be meaningless . . . Certainly in complex societies there is no total social system, that is a social network in which the whole of one's life may be passed, which is also a local territorial unit.'

In discussing the 'communitarian, participatory culture which is really the hunger for Gemeinschaft on a more grandiose scale' (Schel's words), Halsey suggests (p. 150) that 'this kind of sentiment has also found its way . . . into social work'.

Since our research was completed there have been indications of increased interest and sophistication in the patch as a model for service. Hadley and McGrath (1980) identify eleven social services departments which, in one or more teams, have set up patch systems. Their definitions are fairly general (p. 1): 'for the purposes of this bulletin, if you define yourself as a patch system, you are in'. They refer to

the size of population to be served, 'ideally between 5,000–10,000';

orientation to the community and preventive approach;
the implementation of this philosophy by 'maximising autonomy of patch teams', encouraging the use of ancillaries and volunteers 'in responsible roles' and the promotion of co-ordination of work with other agencies, statutory and voluntary.

They have spearheaded what may appropriately be called 'a movement' since it appears for some to carry with it certain ideological overtones. There can be no doubt that there is a tension between the development of patch work and those forms of specialisation which imply a formal concentration of interest upon certain people, problems, or issues. There are important professional and organisational arguments on both sides and these should be distinguished from political dimensions. There are oddities in the political influences which merit some attention, however. On the one hand, advocacy of the patch worker can be associated with the left: its emphasis on the 'humanisation' of the worker, the demystification of professionalism and the opportunity it gives for promoting cohesive social action fit well with this political stance. On the other hand, as has become much more apparent since the Conservatives came to power, the right wing can espouse enthusiastically any system which promotes voluntary effort and the stimulation of caring networks. And it joins with the left in a distrust of professionalism in the 'human relations' field. (Right-wing distrust does not, it seems, extend so far as left-wing distrust does to other areas such as medicine and law.) Clearly, in the climate of the times, this is a powerful, if unexpected and precarious, alliance, and ideologies may obscure the important question – what is the best way of organising services to give people in difficulty the best available help and of contributing to the prevention of these difficulties? The central plank of the argument in favour of the patch system is that it facilitates contact between the social worker and natural helping networks. Hadley and McGrath (1980) argue that what is required to achieve this is a new kind of organisation based on what they call a community-centred model. This model has three features: it is entrepreneurial rather than bureaucratic or professional; it assumes that the community's capacity to care can be increased by appropriate support and that the underlying problems in the area should be identified and dealt with before they result in individual casualties.

There are a number of practical variations on the theme, related to the size of population to be served and number of workers involved – not all those who favour the system insist on one worker per patch. All seem to have in common the use of local paid helpers – street wardens in particular – as well as volunteers. Although, as was suggested earlier, the patch system was favoured by workers in rural areas as more practical in terms of staff deployment, it is in the urban areas that its more sophisticated use has developed.

Two useful contributions carry the debate further. The first, by Thomas and Shaftoe (1974), asks: 'does casework need a neighbourhood orientation?' The second (Currie and Parrott, 1980) gives an account of the application of one form of patch arrangement to the unitary approach. The value of both these lies in their firm roots in practice.

Thomas and Shaftoe tackle definitions (pp. 483–6):

> We understand by the patch or neighbourhood system . . . the decision to divide an area for which a team is responsible into a number of small neighbourhoods, depending on team and population size. A group of workers from the team is then allocated to the neighbourhood or patch.

They say in a footnote that the team described had an establishment of some thirty workers and that the population was 34,000 and add that 'this paper is addressed to a fairly specific type of area and population'. Thus their team was a considerably larger unit than many in other parts of the country, which we found in our study to usually consist of between ten and twelve workers.

It is to be hoped that the terminology used by Thomas and Shaftoe will not add another cluster of infelicitous jargon to social work vocabulary (must we have 'pedestrianised' and 'localisation'?), but the description they offer of the 'friendly neighbourhood social worker' is attractive. There will be, they argue, 'an increase and diversification of the situations in which he meets clients and client groups' and of 'informal social encounters'. The social worker will 'begin to have contact with local residents who are not clients'. The core advantage is that the worker 'has the opportunity to become attached to a defined territory and, hopefully, to become knowledgeable about its culture and committed to its well being'.

> In this way he acquires knowledge of the strengths and resources of the community and may be able to help his clients to utilise them. He is enabled to see his clients functioning effectively in various dimensions of living. He is more exposed to clients' views of the department's sevices. And he has an opportunity to educate the community, for example, in greater tolerance of certain stigmatised groups.

Thomas and Shaftoe do not formally join the anti-professional lobby. They state that these arrangements will help the social worker to 'bring professional services *to people from within the matrix of their own ordinary lives*' (p. 486, their italics). There is nothing inherently inimical to professional behaviour in the proximity which patch systems promote. But it would be naive not to acknowledge the problems that may be created by it which have to be coped with, just as in residential social work. Confidentiality and emotional involvement (the latter being more fundamental than 'the air of skilled detachment' Thomas and Shaftoe mention) are but two of the issues raised by the suggested model, in which the social worker 'eats, drinks and shops . . . locally' and generally enters into the life of the neighbourhood as fully as posible. Furthermore, these activities have somehow to be reconciled with the inescapable elements of social control contained in professional activity. There has been insufficient discussion as yet of these crucial elements. The authors refer to the anxiety which the team felt about the proposed arrangement. 'The issues that aroused most concern were those of effectively using specialist [*sic*] workers in a patch system and of maintaining the work and function of intake teams.' Although this is organisationally important it is interesting that another issue was apparently of less concern – that of having 'less expertise to offer, so that the difficulties of matching skills to needs would be exacerbated'. This illustrates again uncertainty about the status of expertise derived from knowledge and experience of work with specific people or situations and its place in any formal structures. It therefore feeds the enthusiasm of the patch workers, whose claim (quite rightly) to specialist expertise lies in their intimate acquaintance with 'their territory'.

Currie and Parrott (1980) give an able and enthusiastic account of an experiment in one local authority. Its interest goes beyond the patch system *per se* since it attempts to link this to the practice of 'integrated methods'. It carries forward the issues which Bywaters (1978) began to discuss – how to relate the unitary model to the daily work of an area team. There is much in Currie and Parrott's work which merits further debate. Here I focus on its relationship to specialisation.

The experiment described was not pure patch – if such there be – in that an area was divided into three 'identifiable geographical areas' each served by a group of social workers. They argue that patches should be of 'some spatial cohesion' with local offices which are accessible, physically and psychologically. They support Thomas and Shaftoe in the need for the workers to know the locality well and to make themselves known in it.

The collection of data

The extent to which this knowledge is systematically gathered and utilised is an important element in justifying the claim to specialist expertise in the patch. I am not persuaded that poking about in the grass roots is sufficient. Currie and Parrott take 'information-collecting' seriously, citing, *inter alia,* Vickery in support of the view that this model requires careful gathering of local information. Parsloe (1981) outlines the *Guide to the Assessment of Community Needs and Resources* (Glampson *et al.*, 1975) and discusses the attempt of the Harlesden project staff to put this into practice. The information derived from the collection of data from various sources, including the census, housing, education and social services records, forms part of their community analysis. Parsloe stresses the knowledge and skills required for such local research work and suggests that 'social work education may not be preparing students adequately for the task of collecting local information', in particular, experience of surveys is not necessarily the best way to begin. She points out that it may 'require considerable imagination to see *how* to use records and other data' and that the important task of updating is expensive and time-consuming. Yet it is vital because otherwise 'a team may operate for years on what has become inaccurate information'.

Currie and Parrott's approach is less elaborate. Indeed, they stress that 'informal means have probably been the most important'. Specific tasks (for example, reading local council minutes) were delegated to different team members. The style of information-gathering comes over as more informal and emphasis is laid on the understanding of the community through involvement with it, rather than through the collection and analysis of 'hard data'.

Clearly there are important arguments to be resolved in this, the first stage of patch working, that of 'getting to know'. Social workers have been justifiably criticised for lack of precision in many aspects of their work. Certainly one man's flexibility is another man's chaos. And the style of many area teams in social services departments does not give confidence that problems, whether organisational or in the lives of clients, have been grasped purposefully. A first requirement for focused patch work is obviously to have a clear idea of the needs and strengths of a given area, including the likely impact of future trends and developments, and this knowledge is in part available from the data referred to. But if it were to be taken seriously it would surely imply some specialist expertise available, either within or to a team. It is otherwise wasteful of time and resources and may be actually misleading: bluntly, it is not a job for amateurs.

It is, however, easy to see how a preoccupation with fact-gathering could become obsessive, almost an end in itself rather than a means to an end. An absorbing exercise, it could inhibit rather than facilitate action – waiting upon the facts! It seems, *par excellence,* an aspect of work for which guidance from senior management would be valuable. In particular, there should be some agreement as to 'baseline data' which area teams might be expected to collect and to up-date in serving local communities. Recent cuts in research units in social services departments may prove in the longer run wasteful.

One of the helpful consequences of enthusiasm for patch work, then, is the emphasis it places on the gathering of local information, however that may be done. This is an important element in the activity of any area team, whether or not it carries through a patch system of working. Some aspects of it constitute a form of specialism to which skills not integral to social work practice can contribute substantially, for example, in the collection and the analysis of survey data for particular purposes.

The patch and specialism in action

Moving to 'the action', Currie and Parrott do not ignore the specialist/generic tension, although they are confident of the solution. They regret the proliferation of specialist workers and teams which they see as a reaction against generic social work, and maintain that it is possible to reconcile the generic responsibility of a small team for a patch with nearly all specialist needs. They state (p. 18):

> Our argument emphatically does not seek to undervalue specialist skills, specialist methods or the particular needs of certain client groups . . . However, we are not persuaded by arguments . . . against the inclusion of social work services for the 'blind, deaf, handicapped or any other client group within social work teams, given proper access by generic social workers to advice, training and technical support services . . . We reject the argument which moves from 'specialisation' to 'centralisation'. (i.e. outside the patch-based social work activity)

They claim (p. 25) that 'from the basic expectation of a generic workload, specialist interests and responsibilities have developed' and conclude that this 'makes redundant . . . a polarised argument about the merits or demerits of generic social work or specialisation'.

This is a refreshing attempt at reconciliation and it is clear that their 'group/patch' system affords greater flexibility for informal specialisation than the 'individual/patch' arrangements favoured by some. But the problem is not resolved, for the following reasons. First, I am not persuaded that social workers through *informal* specialist interests, combined with other duties, can provide adequate expertise for *all* situations and cases in a given locality. (It is not disputed that it will suffice for some.) This refers back to the fact that some expertise can only be acquired through further professional education, whether in-service or post-qualifying, and through sufficient experience. Although no doubt unintentional, there is, in my view, a kind of arrogance in the assumption that (for example) the problems of some of the physically and mentally handicapped or mentally ill, and their relatives, can be addressed adequately if informal specialism, backed by advice, is all that is offered.

Furthermore – a second problem – a crucial and unresolved question is how the 'advice', training and technical support to which Currie and Parrott refer is made available. Reference was made earlier to our findings that field workers were doubtful about the effectiveness of specialist advisers in offering service to team members. Yet, in a preliminary analysis undertaken at Keele University of how such advisers perceive the weighting of their work, it seems that they see advice to field staff as the primary focus of their work.

I have suggested in Chapter 3 that specialist advice may need to be available at a lower level in the organisation than is customarily the case, that it needs to be shared between teams since no one team can hold all the necessary expertise, and that the role, which has to be formalised to legitimate it, should involve a combination of direct practice with advice if such workers are to be credible. It is not easy to see how such a scheme would fit with the Currie and Parrott model or with that favoured by Goldberg and Warburton (1979). They too advocate a 'broader community and neighbourhood based approach' which would, however, 'make the role of casework more specific'. They continue (p. 134):

> The broad scope of our inquiry makes it difficult to speculate how much specialisation is required at field level in relation to specific client groups . . . What emerged clearly from our study was the need for more accessible specialist consultation *very near field level* [my italics], as Stevenson also found.

The nettle that remains to be grasped by those who value neighbourhood work but accept the necessity for other specialist skills is basically an organisational one. Who is to work where, with whom, in what role? What is the proper balance between the two? There will not be a blueprint, given the diversity of need and of community characteristics. But the need to experiment and to monitor carefully experiments that seek to provide a neighbourhood service which includes specialist workers seems essential if the argument is to be constructively moved on and more than lip service is to be paid to the value of specialist skills.

The third difficulty in the argument concerns an implicit assumption of the proponents of patch work that caring networks can be stimulated through neighbourhood work. Whilst this will undoubtedly be true in some places and for some clients, it cannot be assumed it holds good for all. For example, the street network may be crucial and effective for some elderly people: for some of the relatives of the mentally handicapped or physically disabled community support, especially self-help groups, may be better mobilised across a wider geographical area. There are dangers of unreality in too inclusive a notion of neighbourhood networks. Indeed, for some potential clients, it may be positively unacceptable. Thus there is a fine balance between the advantages of 'spin-off' from one group to another, to which Currie and Parrott refer, and the help which certain individuals and groups need to be linked in to networks outside their 'territory'.

Fourthly, which leads to the next main area for discussion, there is the tension between the local focus and the need for structures which facilitate interprofessional work. Currie and Parrott accept the importance of this and describe the ways in which patch workers created attachments to specific institutions, such as schools, for this purpose. Organisational difficulties, however, are likely to be considerable. It is a fortunate chance if the 'territories' agreed by the workers as having 'spatial cohesion' coincide with the major centres, such as hospitals and schools, with which the social workers must relate. In my view, this is one of the major unresolved difficulties in developing appropriate models for service delivery and merits attention in considerable detail.

(B) ASPECTS OF INTERPROFESSIONAL CO-OPERATION

Is it essential?

The arrangements made for communication, co-operation and collaboration between social workers and others, potentially or actually, involved with the same clients reopens a consideration of the nature of the social work task. Some writers (for example, Webb and Hobdell, 1980; Parsloe, 1981) seem to imply that the time spent on such work is in a sense optional and its value has to be balanced against time spent on other elements of practice. Webb and Hobdell (p. 109) ask:

> Should we forget the problems of co-ordination – with the exception of a few especially sensitive issues such as that of children at risk of physical harm – and *concentrate on raising the professional standard of social work?* [my italics]. This latter course would conceivably do more for collaboration between doctors and social workers than hastily improvised structures and procedures designed to induce the early birth of mutual professional accord and effective communication.

Parsloe discusses Parker's (1980) 'model of the market place' and his suggestion that

> co-operation needs to be seen as a transaction in which time, knowledge, prestige, power or money may be being moved

from one organisation to another . . . in which the outcomes may not be equally advantageous for all parties.

Parker suggests that the level of co-operation will be determined, *inter alia,* by 'the costs of failure' and that 'any organisation can only handle a finite amount of co-operation'. Parsloe adds: 'I suspect that each individual also has a limit . . . since the processes are intellectually and emotionally demanding.' She 'throws some doubt on the assumption that co-operation is an end in itself'.

A further dimension to the argument is, of course, the extent to which co-operation rather than conflict is perceived to be the more useful for the client. Currie and Parrott (1980) allude, cautiously, to this: if the patch workers get too cosy with local officials and professionals it could, in some circumstances, act against the interests of the client. At this point ideological disputes about the role of the social worker creep in. My assumption is that the client is best served *at a local level* by efforts at inter-professional co-operation, provided his needs, and not the comfort of the workers, are central and that, if such efforts fail, the confrontation is sophisticated. As Currie and Parrott sensibly remark (p. 10): 'At times it is necessary to use leverage, but knowledge of the organisation is essential in deciding when to apply pressure, how to apply it and at what points.'

The arguments raised by Webb and Hobdell and Parsloe do not seem to me to include an acceptable view of the core of the social work task. I would argue that the arrangements made for communication, co-operation and collaboration between social workers and others actually or potentially involved with the same clients are crucial for effective social work service. It is commonplace to write about the interdependence and interaction of the physical, social and psychological aspects of human functioning and numerous writers have stressed that social work is concerned with the quality of life at these interfaces. Yet the implications for the definition of this task have not been followed through. To stake a claim for expertise at such meeting points is no more arrogant than is that of the general practitioner to make links between the sub-systems of his client's body which different specialists may treat. The social worker does not know as much as the doctor about the health of the parents, nor as much as the health visitor about the dietary needs of his young children or the teacher about the educational needs of his older children. But his task is to see the connections between these facets of a family's life and to effect what changes he can to enhance the functioning of its members. The reality of social work activity in this country, except for the most unusual (some would say precious), has always been thus. The fantasy of the social worker as psychotherapist has taken an unconscionably long time a-dying, as Butrym (1976) points out. Indeed the fantasy may perhaps be more accurately described as a straw man! Studies of social work activity have shown the high proportion of social work time taken up with activities which involve contact with persons other than the client. For example, Goldberg and Warburton (1979, pp. 75ff., table 8:2) describe the work coming into Seatown's area teams. Their case review system enabled categories of work to be analysed. In only 17 per cent of nearly 2,000 cases handled was there no contact made with outside agencies. Jeans (1979), borrowing terminology from the USA, analysed social work activity in hospitals and area teams, under thirteen heads, of which six are clearly concerned with this aspect, to a greater or lesser degree. These are: linking; advocacy; mobilising resources; offering consultation; teaching; co-ordination. In an admittedly modest quantitative analysis of the number of such contacts, all, but especially the first three, played a significant part. Goldberg and Warburton's work referred to above confirms this. In their analysis, 40 per cent of cases required information and advice and 36 per cent required mobilisation of resources. Thus, whether or not direct contact was made with other agencies, knowledge of what they had to offer was vital in a large number of cases.

Thus, if we ask 'what is the daily bread and butter of social work activity as presently constituted?', the answer is as much to do with seeing *about* clients as seeing them. It does not, of course, follow that what presently happens is a proper use of social worker time. Indeed, Goldberg and Warburton use the data obtained to argue (p. 134) that much social work time is unprofitably expended on such tasks and 'there is much room for' specialisation in gate-keeping functions, 'which would not necessarily be performed by social workers'. I shall return to this in the next chapter. But I find it impossible to conceive of effective social work in which contact and relationships with people other than the client do not continue to occupy much of the centre of the stage. In fact if the boundaries of social work and, in particular, casework were more tightly drawn, the need for closer collaborative activity would if anything be increased.

'Attachment' as a means of co-operation

Such observations will of course be warmly acclaimed by some of those in other occupational groups who see this in simplistic terms. 'Attach a social worker to us', they cry, 'and all will be well.' Would it were so easy. Attachment can take various forms, from a full-time worker based in the agency to part-time arrangements in which the worker 'visits' regularly but may not even have a physical base on the premises. Hospital social workers are the clearest example of the former: many social workers operate schemes of the latter type, with schools and health centres, from the base of their area team.

Any attachment from an area team which is on the full-time, agency-based end of the continuum raises three problems.

First, attachments to particular institutions are not necessarily the most efficient way of deploying scarce social work resources. It is logistically complex. Such arrangements can be made for a time where there is a special job to be done. The justification for permanent attachment has to be more carefully weighed. Should it be all the schools or only some? All the general practices or only some? What about key institutions in a particular neighbourhood, such as juvenile courts? Goldberg and Neill (1972) explore the issue of attachment in relation to general practice at the conclusion of an important experiment. They argue (p. 174–5):

> Surveys so far carried out . . . and our own experience suggests that there is ample scope for experiment with different forms of liaison between general practice and social work, including secondment and attachment. It would be a great pity if the attachment of social workers to general practice were to lead to a concept of 'my social worker' and inhibit more general and direct collaboration between general practitioners, social workers and other helpers in the community.

Thus they seem to be suggesting that more flexible arrangements than a full-time attachment may pay off better.

Secondly, there is a long-standing problem about the authority which one group assumes over another which may become more apparent when they are working closely together. This is discussed by Kane (1975) in her review of interprofessional teamwork and discussed by several authors in Lonsdale, Webb and Briggs (1980). The relationship between doctors and social workers offers the most obvious example and is well illustrated both by the position of many hospital social workers and by the difficulties which have occurred between psychiatrists and 'new-style' generic social workers, whose approach to compulsory admissions has in some instances differed from that of their old-time equivalents, the mental welfare officers. The problem is not exclusively centred on these professions, however. Education welfare officers, retained by the education departments at the point of reorganisation of the personal social services, have paid the price of continuing difficulty in establishing their occupational status within the schools.

The decision to separate health and social services at local level, deplored by many doctors and some social workers at the time, has created the need for new structures to ensure co-operation. In time, however, it may become apparent that the decision has played a significant part in achieving a more appropriate balance of power between the two services. Excessive fragmentation of area teams through extensive 'attachments' could undermine the progress which, in my view, there has been. This progress – and its halting steps – is shown in the evolution of case conference procedures in cases of child abuse. It was symbolised by the conference attended by the present author at which, it subsequently transpired, participants were unsure whether doctor or social worker was the chairman! (Hallett and Stevenson, 1980).

There is a third difficulty about full-time attachment which is equally important and perhaps more subtle than the familiar one of real and perceived authority. That is the general problem which any occupational group has in preserving its identity, expressed in terms of values and objectives, when individual workers are separated from their reference point and placed in relative isolation within host organisations. This was vividly shown in the course of a project, directed by the present author, in which one social worker was placed in each of seven supplementary benefits offices to act in a role comparable with that of unemployment review officers. In the course of this experiment, which lasted a year, the social workers, although glad about their increased understanding of the role and difficulties of supplementary benefits officials, became anxious about the extent to which certain attitudes which they did not respect towards the unemployed were creeping, unwelcomed, into their own work (Stevenson, 1973). Numbers are important. Clearly the fewer 'outsiders', the more significant the impact on them when within an alien institution.

This is not intended to suggest there is no place for full-time attachment from area teams. It is simply to point out some of its complexities, as we struggle to formulate patterns of working which balance different organisational and professional constraints.

Factors involved in interprofessional work

There are two dimensions to the 'three Cs' of communication, co-operation and collaboration which have to be taken into account. One is to ensure effective transactions which benefit the client who has been defined as in need of service. The second is to foster relationships which will make early and appropriate referral (in all directions) more likely. The first facilitates the second but the closer the working relationships (provided, of course, there is reasonable harmony), the more sensitive the referrals will be. Thus arrangements which encourage communication over and above that concerned with a particular case are likely to be necessary if 'preventive' work is to be developed.

The range of connections which social workers must make concerning particular cases is wide, their nature varied and the persons with whom the social worker communicates differ greatly in their roles and associated status. Parker (1980) has provided a useful diagram (adapted here in Figure 4.1) to suggest groupings which might form a basis for specialisation). A further complication is that contact is necessary with different agencies, officials, or professionals at different times and that these contacts may vary in intensity over time. Attachment to a particular agency, therefore, does not necessarily offer an easy solution.

Figure 4.1 Area teams – necessary connections.

Note: Employment services are not included.

Three aspects of interaction can be distinguished: its purpose, frequency and duration. Taking the actual (rather than the potential) case as the focus, the purpose of the interaction may be: to pass on or exchange information (communication); to request action; to share risks (as in child abuse case conferences); to decide on a prime worker or co-ordinator (co-operation); to plan and co-ordinate treatment (collaboration). Any one of these activities may create single, occasional, or frequent contact and may range from an isolated episode to prolonged contact over years. Furthermore, as has been suggested earlier, interaction to identify a potential case requires the creation of a climate in which referrals may spontaneously arise.

This has been a long-standing, intractable problem in relationships between supplementary benefits officials and social workers and was examined in detail by the present author (Stevenson, 1973). The officials had a duty to refer cases needing 'welfare' but the motivation and knowledge to do so efficiently were often missing. (What will happen following the radical changes in the supplementary benefits scheme introduced in 1980 remains to be seen.)

The required interactions are diverse and complex. The 'Parker diagram', however, suggests certain natural groupings and the idea of moving from communication through co-operation to collaboration may give a framework for devising the minimum necessary conditions for effective transactions.

Specialisation in relation to the 'three Cs'

The case for specialisation becomes stronger as we move along these three dimensions. Thus it is not the client group *per se* but the complexity of a specific case measured by the *nature and frequency* of the interactions required with other professions and officials which may lead to allocation to a specialist. This is not, of course, the only reason. We are discussing here one variable – but a crucial one. Whilst it may be more common for one type of case to present this dimension of complexity than another, it is by no means clear-cut. Thus, a mentally handicapped adult may be stable within his family in the community and well supported so that there is little need for liaison with other professions; whereas a severely mentally handicapped child in a family with other problems may require intensive collaborative activity between a number of experts. This activity is not only time-consuming: if co-operation and collaboration are to be achieved, a degree of trust and mutual confidence has to be established and this is likely to be fostered if the social worker has contact with the other professionals concerning more than one case and demonstrates a grasp of the salient points to those professionals who are themselves 'specialists'; for example, to the teacher at a school for handicapped children. Thus tentatively we move towards one possible criterion for specialisation of task – when certain cases require close and/or intensive interprofessional relationships for efficient service to be given.

Before such a suggestion can be taken much further, however, an analysis is required of the numbers and types of such cases which come, *or should come*, to the social services department for social work service. (It is not enough simply to study what comes already; we know that many of those in need of the help social work can and should offer are not referred to social services departments.)

Whilst there would be some professional dispute as to where the line should be drawn, a careful assessment of existing cases could be made on the basis of their 'co-operative' complexity. This could be done in a given area by a careful review of existing cases and by asking other relevant professionals and officials to join in an assessment of newly referred or 'would like to have referred' cases. This would admittedly not catch those where the other professionals did not value social work but, if carefully explained to those participating as an exercise designed to assess the need for different co-operative structures, it would be useful and it would avoid the fear of raising client expectations unrealistically.

Such information would go further than the Goldberg and Warbuton (1979) data, valuable though these are. Their analysis of 'a year's intake to an area office' provides material essential to any description of an area team's work, in terms of the types of people and problems who came to

'Seatown'. Since only a small proportion (about 6 per cent) of the 2,000 case studies were receiving continuous social work help six months after referral (p. 69), it is obvious that very few were receiving help through intensive interprofessional activity. That, however, says nothing about whether they should have been receiving such help. The evidence, from our research and elsewhere, points to the likelihood that much interprofessional activity will be lacking in those aspects of social work service which have 'low visibility' in social services departments. Unfortunately many of those clients, including some of the elderly and handicapped, are precisely those for whom such co-operation is particularly important. In child abuse cases strenuous efforts have been made to ensure more effective interprofessional work. And, in general, it is well known that long-term child and family cases usually require extensive contact with outside agencies. Goldberg and Warburton (1979, p. 106, table 11:2) show that in such cases, for example, 51 per cent required contact with the education service, 32 per cent with courts and solicitors, 20 per cent with the police, though the frequency and nature of these contacts are not mapped. So, if one puts together what happens and what perhaps should happen, it seems certain that a substantial proportion of individuals and families have problems in which close collaboration with other professionals or officials is at the core of effective social work intervention. It is argued here that it cannot be 'optional' and that social workers bear a particular responsibility for the creation and sustaining of structures and relationships which will seek to achieve it, which implies some form of specialisation.

Chapter 5

The Organisation of Work (II)

(A) THE STRUCTURE OF TEAMS

So far we have discussed only two of the variables which were outlined earlier as having to be balanced in the decisions taken regarding specialisation. Other factors relating to the organisation of work are now considered. Parsloe, in this series (1981), discusses many aspects of the team as a unit of service delivery. Here the analysis is of one particular issue, that of specialisation, and should be taken as complementary to that discussion. There are two general points of particular relevance to our theme.

First, the size of the team greatly affects the possibilities for specialisation. Is the typical team in social services departments, comprising eight to ten staff of whom perhaps six are social workers, too small to cover sufficient areas of formal planned specialisation? Given the difficulty which, as we found in our study, teams have in sharing colleagues with other teams, it may be that a necessary pre-condition for the development of effective specialisation is a larger unit of service than is at present usual.

Secondly, even such larger units do not preclude the possibility of certain specialised teams (rather than sub-teams) operating from another location. But the purposes of those developments have implications for the total pattern of social work service and need to be carefully considered. I return to this later.

Key factors in team structure

What are the key factors of which one needs to take account in the organisation of social work service within a team? These may be divided into the inescapable 'facts of life' which confront social workers in an area team and the professional possibilities which some would wish to take into account in planning work. Both are relevant for they may lead to different forms of work division which relate to specialisation.

First, then, 'the facts of life'. These concern the flow of referrals, their number, nature and relative urgency; the widely differing ongoing needs of clients; the pressures for action in respect of certain cases both from within the organisation and from outside, from other professionals and the local community. Every team must make an organisational response to the way in which work presents itself. Thus, for example, arrangements for 'duty', however rudimentary, are universal. A vital consideration concerns the interplay between professional values and organisational efficiency. It would be comforting to believe that these are likely to be congruent, but it cannot be assumed that efficiency relates to the values to which the organisation is seemingly committed. In particular, when a necessary objective – that of protecting the worker against too much stress – becomes too dominant, the flow of work may be organised in a way positively inimical to professional values. Hall (1974), for example, has shown how the receptionist's role affects, and is affected by, the workers' need to be shielded from clients. Accepting, therefore, that interaction of organisation upon the quality of social work service needs constantly to be monitored, and that there will be both immediate and longer-term effects, what are the effects of certain forms of specialisation upon these interactions?

'Duty', short-term work and 'crisis' work

Two aspects of the work are inter-related but separate. One concerns 'duty', the way incoming work is received. The other concerns 'short-term' work. Rowlings, in our research (Chapter V), showed how varied were the practices and styles of 'duty officers', even within teams. There are clearly problems in ensuring an appropriate quality of service at this crucial initial contact: factors such as lack of skill in initial interviewing and of commitment to transient work which may be seen as an unwelcome interruption have to be taken into account.

'Brief work' is significant to most social services teams for two reasons. First, there seems little doubt that a high proportion of the work coming to the teams is of short duration (Goldberg and Warburton, 1979). Secondly, research into and discussion of short-term casework (Reid and Shyne, 1969; Reid and Epstein, 1972), sometimes linked to the notion of 'contract', has generated professional interest (and dare one say also lent an air of respectability?) to an area of work previously little discussed.

These factors have combined to encourage the development of intake teams, probably the most common form of 'internal' social work specialisation. (In one month alone, January 1979, thirty-two posts advertised in *Social Work Today* were for workers in intake.) There are many different patterns of 'intake', which is not synonymous with 'duty', and a number of articles have appeared describing these. Rowlings, in our study (p. 51), sums up a number of the difficulties identified by our respondents and others (see, for example, Social Services Study Group, 1979):

> The proportion of staff to be deployed on intake rather than long term work; the level of experience and qualification held by intake workers; the place of staff without a CQSW qualification; the definition of long and short term; and the transfer of work between teams.

The Social Services Study Group (1979, p. 44) suggest that, from their survey, the problems most often mentioned about intake teams 'relate to staff experience rather than service provision'. Goldberg and Warburton (1979), supporting this view, are perhaps the strongest critics of intake systems, though a general air of disillusionment has been evident in recent literature. They point out (p. 125) that

> in the very group in which social workers reported most casework activity, namely amongst those experiencing family and child care problems, dissatisfaction was greater and complaints more numerous than among the elderly and those with material problems . . . Their reasons did not seem so much related to social class and cultural gaps *as to lack of experience and of specialised knowledge and skills and time pressures* . . .

[my italics]. One is tempted to speculate that in the pressured atmosphere of an intake team concerned with continuous screening, 'one-off advice' and the delivery of a wide variety of practical services, *careful exploration and assessment, . . . one of the most important keys to successful social work intervention . . . may be in danger of atrophy* (My italics).

The authors wish to see social work time differently and more economically used, a point to which I shall return in the next chapter. But it is evident that, in 'Seatown', there was considerable 'slippage' between the notions of duty and short-term work. The original, rather sophisticated, intention of an intake process was one in which 'careful exploration and assessment' were at the heart of the enterprise. This seems to have been frustrated, whether by 'bombardment' or by inadequate understanding is not clear. In fact, in intake work, there is a distinction to be drawn between three elements; first, *new* work, secondly, *crisis* work and thirdly, *short-term* work. Examination of different patterns of intake shows that all three are not necessarily present in a particular intake team. For example (although this is probably unusual), one intake team in our study did not 'do duty' and were thus free to concentrate upon short-term work. It is in any case by no means self-evident that planned short-term work is psychologically or practically difficult to combine with sustained long-term work and it is well recognised that, when they are divided, difficulties over the manner and timing of transfer from short to long term do arise. A more subtle problem, difficult to combat, concerns the prestige with which, it seems, certain kinds of work are at times invested. Both 'short' and 'long' have at different times acquired this prestige. It is clearly unprofitable if it carries with it the inference that work with certain clients whose need is for long-term or short-term social work is less skilled. The dangers are too obvious to merit discussion.

The other two elements, of new and crisis work, involve different considerations. The need for special arrangements to deal with the former will depend to a large extent on sheer volume. But, as will be discussed later, the development of certain practices, procedures and skills with regard to assessment may be given impetus by a degree of specialisation, especially since these involve a team as a whole, from receptionist to senior social worker. The demands of what can superficially be described as crisis work deserve more precise consideration. There is a need for a new word to describe, quite simply, a sudden, unpredictable demand for social work services rather than a traumatic episode in an individual's life. The two may coincide but they are quite distinct. To confuse them does not help social workers to separate theory underpinning therapeutic intervention from organisational arrangements which affect professional practice.

Crisis theory (Parad, 1965) is concerned with loss and with the grieving, normal and pathological, which follows it. Traumatic events, such as bereavement, precipitate a crisis. Such a formulation may exclude many 'self-induced' crises; for example, the trials and tribulations of a so-called 'problem family', though frequently described as 'crises', do not come within the definition. (This is an area, however, in which the literature is somewhat obscure. What about attempted suicide, for example?) If the theoretical framework is unclear, the use of the term 'crisis' to describe simply sudden happenings which call for action in a social services department is unhelpful. These 'happenings' range from the trivial to the serious; their only common characteristic is that, for one reason or another, they demand immediate action. The apparently trivial may, of course, generate anxiety in clients disproportionate to the event, dealing with which requires a high order of social work skill. Or they may be trivial (a lost purse) in comparison with other matters (an injured child) but pose a problem which is serious in the sense that a basic need for food must be met immediately. What they all have in common, however, is that they disrupt the planned work of social services staff who must attend to them.

There are some individuals and families whose need for service is predictable in its unpredictability. This has been graphically described by Mattinson and Sinclair (1979) whose work with a group of such families, although focused on marital difficulties, took them into many dimensions of the clients' social functioning.

The authors argue (p. 293) that 'we had, as a starting point to offer them a *limited, reliable and defined contact*' (original italics). They suggest (p. 296) that

> the resources of the social work division of the department in which we worked were heavily concentrated on a group of clients whose emotional problems related to disturbed attachment and actual and feared losses. An appropriate treatment for such clients requires, as a start, the offer of a limited attachment relationship. This presupposes time and reliability on the part of the social workers, which were difficult to offer within the existing context, structure and responsibilities of the area offices.

Mattinson and Sinclair point out that even if the intensive work which they undertook is not attempted (p. 297), 'the statutory requirements and community pressures ensure that this group of clients cannot be left alone'.

It is likely that work with such families would create intolerable anxiety in some workers and that few could sustain the intensity of the involvement required indefinitely. But implicit in Mattinson and Sinclair's account of their work is a conviction that such families can be helped, in ways which are seemingly more time-consuming but which may ultimately prove more economical if their demands are 'held' by specialist workers. This affords a welcome contrast to the gloomy account in Goldberg and Warburton (1979, p. 108) of long-term social work with child and family problems, which concludes: 'This group of chronic family problems raises many questions about the residual functions of the social services departments which cannot refuse to take on cases at risk, however impervious they may be to social work intervention.'

Goldberg and Warburton argue (p. 130) in their conclusion for more effective use of task-centred casework with such families. Whilst not wishing to detract from the value of this method, in the light of the work of Mattinson and Sinclair, and indeed of many Family Service Units over many years, a specialism which ensures appropriate professional availability, sometimes over a number of years but with focused, purposeful intervention as a prerequisite, is arguably just as appropriate. There is fertile ground for further research.

There is, however, a further question – whether such 'crisis-engendering' individuals and families could form a specialist unit, even a dyad, which could cut across conventional client groupings. This might include the following:

- a couple with a marital problem, involving violence and temporary separation;
- a schizophrenic, at home with parents, prone to episodes of disturbing behaviour;
- an elderly woman, suffering from senile dementia, whose behaviour provokes complaints from neighbours;
- a teenager with a drink problem;
- a family whose financial problems lead to frequent emergency requests for help.

The viability of such a grouping depends, as do so many ways of organising work, upon expertise available to workers on particular aspects of certain cases, for example, on senile dementia or alcoholism. However, it might lead to an interesting extension of social work skill and technique, through the concentration upon the response to seemingly urgent 'happenings', with an increased understanding of 'trigger factors' and of ways of responding helpfully.

The above is an example of specialisation which is related directly to the nature of the work that presents itself to an area team. In industrial terms it is 'operative specialisation' and can only be justified if it appears to provide an as good or a better service to clients. Much will depend upon the work-flow. It might, however, improve the quality of service to the long-term, 'steadier' clients if their care were not so disrupted by the 'urgent few'.

Division of work by client group

Much more common in practice has been the emergence of divisions of work between what are often called 'family and child care' and 'health and/or social care', the latter usually including the elderly. These may be separate from area teams or 'teams within teams'. Often the word 'family' is omitted from the description of the latter team. This is unfortunate but probably significant. It seems to imply an emphasis on family interaction in the one and not in the other, whereas, of course, in a substantial number of cases, family processes are equally important. Thus the emergence of such teams may be a mixed blessing. On the one hand, there are strong arguments for the creation of specialised units if they give the impetus to this area of work to balance the conspicuous domination of 'children's work' and if they provide a better framework for interprofessional co-operation. On the other hand, if *social work* service (as distinct from *social service* provision) is explicitly or implicitly less valued, this is deplorable. Much will depend on the composition of the team, above all its leadership.

Nor is it obviously logical to group together clients whose only common feature is that they are not 'statutory child care'. The range of problems, if cases involving mental or physical illness or handicap and the elderly are lumped together, is diverse. The case of a family with a mentally handicapped child, in which, for example, the siblings are showing signs of distressed behaviour, will have more in common with that of a family where a child is emotionally disturbed than with the case of a frail elderly person living alone. The profession needs organisational structures which facilitate the transfer of relevant knowledge.

In any specialist division of labour the needs of the frail elderly merit particular consideration. The contribution of patch work to this group is of particular importance: this style of work is bound up with the use of 'indigenous' helpers, whether paid or unpaid, and an intimate knowledge and stimulation of the street-by-street networks may afford one of the best protections of the frail elderly in the community. Given the size and nature of the problem which confronts us in supporting such elderly persons and those who provide their basic care, it seems certain that a major part of social services activity must be directed towards the co-ordination of community effort. As Currie and Parrott (1980) suggest, a generic service to a given locality may well throw up benefits, sometimes unexpected, across client groupings, especially if the client can also be a helper. Neighbourhood work with the elderly is therefore likely to benefit other people besides the elderly and, conversely, the elderly will benefit from social work relationships with other people in the locality.

As with all other groups, however, some structures have to be created to ensure that their special needs and problems are taken as seriously, and met as skilfully, as those of others; this has not been the case so far with the elderly. The number and nature of the needs presented by the elderly seem to indicate a different approach from that for the younger handicapped or mentally ill, since for nearly all of these and for their relatives there is a traumatic point at which skilled assessment of complex interacting factors is important. The problems of the frail elderly often emerge gradually. That does not, however, make the review of their situation and careful assessment at certain stages less important (Rowlings, 1981). Furthermore for the elderly too there are the inevitable life crises, especially of bereavement, and the major problem of mental deterioration is another matter where expert advice on management may be essential. Enthusiasm for the mobilisation of community support, therefore, must not overshadow the recognition of the need for such expertise in casework with the elderly and their carers, an issue which is ably explored in depth by Rowlings (1981). It seems likely that the sheer numbers involved in most places will make it necessary to have some form of specialist in direct work as well as in 'community care'.

In Chapter 7 a suggestion of a possible model will be outlined, in which an attempt is made to meet each of the points discussed here, for and against a specialist 'health care team', with or without the elderly. However, more experiments, carefully monitored, are essential. It is only through experience that we shall be able to offer guidelines as to which patterns in which areas provide the most effective service. (The present author is currently directing DHSS-funded research into this, with special reference to the physically disabled.)

In particular, further consideration needs to be given to the structures most suitable to provide area teams with adequate advice and support; whether they operate with generic caseloads or with specialist sub-teams they need this. Area teams are unlikely in the foreseeable future to have within them adequate services from medical or paramedical personnel, valuable as these would be.

The use of hospital teams already in existence is one possibility. Could they reach out farther into the community in offering systematic support and advice to area teams? A further contribution, discussed in the next chapter, might be the use of residential care staff, especially those caring for the handicapped, ill and elderly, to advise social workers on problems of management encountered by families.

However it is worked out, it is clear that social services teams, as presently constituted, should not 'go it alone'. In child abuse, systems of co-ordination involving all the relevant professionals have been devised through the machinery of area review committees. The case conference has been an important element in this. A good case could be made out for some similar arrangements whereby certain cases are selected for assessment and some for ongoing review by an interprofessional group. This practice is well established within certain hospital teams. There are many cases which do not involve hospital care which would profit from this kind of interprofessional activity.

One suggestion currently finding favour in some social services departments is that of the 'district handicap team' to which Browne (1979) refers. One authority suggests a pilot project for such a development in relation to children. Browne describes their outline as follows:

(1) *Core Team:*
paediatrician of first contact (that is, the consultant to whom the patient is referred);
paediatric sister or the sister in charge of the special care baby unit (dependent on the ward in which the infant is placed);
paediatric social worker;
educational psychologist;

administrative support team.

(2) *Extended team:*
health visitor;
general practitioner;
senior clinical medical officer;
community social worker.

(3) *Support team:*
additional professional support according to the needs of individual children; for example orthopaedic surgeon, physiotherapist, child psychiatrist, speech therapist, advisory teacher, etc.

The Core Team members would be named practitioners who would thus build up a regular working relationship and they would be the permanent element in the network. Each would be responsible for ensuring the initial professional input from his own discipline.

The co-ordinator would be the paediatrician who, having the vital role of diagnosis of the medical condition and of informing the parents, would then bring the district handicap team together.

The special nursing element would be assessed and initially provided by the particular nursing sister of the ward involved.

The paediatric social worker would assess the social needs of the child and family.

The educational psychologist would advise on the educational needs of the child.

(The special nursing element would obviously not be required in every case, for example, with older emotionally disturbed children.)

The Extended Team members would be the particular practitioners involved with the child and his family. They would be essentially community-based and concerned with meeting the family's needs in that community.

The Support Team members would provide the specific professional expertise that was required to meet the identified needs of a particular child. They would be co-opted as and when necessary and could be either hospital- or community-based.

The team would concern itself with children suffering from severe physical and mental handicaps.

The *key worker* will be nominated by the team.

It was suggested that such a team could use various agencies, according to the nature of the problem, as bases for operations. These could include the local hospital, child guidance clinics, observation and assessment centres, or day nurseries.

The idea of such a district handicap team will not appeal to everyone nor suit the varied circumstances of all social services departments. This example is quoted simply to emphasise the importance of the structures which may be devised outside area teams to provide expertise and support to them.

(B) NEED FOR SPECIALISATION AS PERCEIVED BY SOCIAL SERVICES DEPARTMENTS

The fourth factor which has affected the development of specialisation in the past decade is the 'felt need' for certain specialisms, either because of the skills required, or (more commonly) because of the need to develop certain skills or resources. One way of assessing what has been happening is to examine the advertisements which have appeared in the journals. The 'snapshot' which follows is probably fairly typical; it is certainly in line with the informal communications which I have received.

Recent trends in formal specialisation

Tables 5.1 to 5.3 are based on an analysis of posts available in area teams or of direct relevance to them, within social services departments, which were advertised in *Social Work Today* in January 1979. They have been divided, conventionally, into two groupings, those concerned with 'child care' and those with 'health and the elderly', and are compared with other area-based posts. The total number of posts taken into account does not include residential or administrative posts, nor 'social work' posts in agencies other than social services departments.

Table 5.1 *'Child care' posts advertised in Social Work Today, January 1979*

Type of work	Grade of post		
	Senior and above	Social worker	Totals
Fostering and/or adoption	5	16	21
Intermediate treatment	1	10	11
Court work	1	2	3
IT/court work	—	2	2
NAI/'intensive care'	2	6	8
'Under 5s'	—	5	5
Schools	—	2	2
Child minding	—	2	2
General/other	16	33	49
Totals	25	78	103

'Child care' posts: 103
Overall total: 293
Percentage of 'child care' posts 35·2%

Certain interesting points emerge from Table 5.1. First, two specialisms, for fostering and adoption and intermediate treatment, are part of a national trend. Together they formed about one-third of the child care specialisms and far outnumbered any other within that group except for those whose specialism was broadly 'child care duties', a category which comprised very nearly half of these specialist posts. Otherwise there was a scatter of interests; perhaps surprisingly, there was no marked trend towards specialist posts for treatment of child abuse.

The predominance of a fostering and adoption specialism seems to reflect the renewed impetus given to these forms of placement in the 1970s and is an interesting example of the sustained and organised influence of certain pressure groups, in particular the Association of British Adoption and Fostering Agencies and what might be described as 'the fostering lobby', active at the time the Children Bill was before Parliament. The progress of that Bill, before its enactment in 1975, was in turn affected by the reverberations of the report of the Maria Colwell inquiry (Colwell Report 1974). It is to expected, indeed hoped, that professional values and attitudes will be affected by research. Nor should the impact of social pressures, embodied in various groups and organisations, be undervalued. However, the need for the specialists to be relatively sophisticated about the implications of research becomes all the more important if social work is not to sway before every wind. Thus the case for post-qualifying studies of various kinds and readily available help in the evaluation of research is strengthened by the creation of these specialisms. The quality of the work is not necessarily improved simply by the creation of the posts.

The advertisements do not give a clear indication of the scope and responsibilities of these adoption and fostering posts. This is important in determining the relationship between generic and specialist workers. Are the latter primarily concerned to find and to assess prospective parents and to make linkages with social workers who have children in need of substitute care? Or do they extend their role into placement and, if so, how are links with the original social worker (and, if relevant, with the parents of the child) maintained? Or are they more concerned to forge relationships with residential staff to cater for the 'children who wait'? More information on the ways such posts are being developed is needed.

As was discussed in our research, the growth of 'intermediate treatment' as a specialism is an interesting example of what might be described as 'legitimating through legislation'. The use of the term, borrowed from the Children and Young Persons Act 1969, somehow lends respectability to what was previously often called 'youth and community work' and, of course, it was brought into the framework of social services provision. This is not to cast doubt on the value of some of the innovative work which has thereby been done. It is simply to illustrate the political and social factors which influence the profession.

Table 5.2 *'Elderly and health' posts advertised in Social Work Today, January 1979*

Type of work	Grade of post		
	Senior and above	Social worker	Totals
Elderly	3	1	4
Elderly/physically handicapped	5	5	10
Physically handicapped	1	3	4
Deaf	—	2	2
Blind	—	1	1
Physical and mental health	—	2	2
Health liaison	1 (Principal)	—	1
Mentally ill	1	7	8
Mentally handicapped	4	5	9
Mental illness and handicap	2	1	3
GP attachment	—	1	1
General hospital and area	—	1	1
Psychiatric hospital and area	—	1	1
Totals	17	32	49

'Elderly and health' posts: 49
Overall total: 293
Percentage of 'elderly and health' posts: 16·7%

Moving to Table 5.2 on 'elderly and health', it is to be noted that the percentage of special posts advertised in the same month was 16·7 as compared with 35·2 for children and families. No specialisms are clearly much more significant than others; in fact, the percentage for workers with the elderly and handicapped, with the mentally handicapped and with the mentally ill constitute about one-fifth each of the whole. The variations upon the theme, that is, the ways in which the group is sub-divided, are more interesting than overall numbers.

Table 5.3 *'Other area-based posts' advertised in* Social Work Today, *January 1979*

Type of work	Grade of post		
	Senior and above	Social worker	Totals
Community work	3	4	7
Ethnic minorities	—	3	3
Welfare rights	—	1	1
Intake	12	20	32
Long-term/generic	9	14	23
Generic/patch	—	18	18
Generic + 'opportunities to specialise'	2	36	38
Emergency duty	5	14	19
Totals	31	110	141

'Other area-based posts': 141
Overall total: 293
Percentage of 'other' posts: 48.1%

Table 5.3 offers a comparison between formal specialisation and generic work. Looking at the figures as percentages of the 293 posts taken into account, about 27 per cent were generic, though nearly half of them (13 per cent in all) offered informal opportunities to specialise. Approximately 17 per cent of all the posts were for specialists relating to the division of work, in intake or emergency duty teams. In some of these advertisements, the opportunity to work a patch system is specifically mentioned.

Although the advertisements have been analysed with reference to the usual client group specialisms, it should be noted that a number elaborate on these, either by reference to method (for example, 'opportunities to develop group-work or family therapy'), by attachment to a particular institution, or by reference to projects (for example, to develop for the elderly an experimental community-based service). The vast majority, however, remained 'pinned' to client groups. Thus it can be seen that specialism, according to the needs perceived by social services departments, is broadly emerging within the framework of conventional groupings, although more unusual or sophisticated sub-categories may be found within them. That these are much more evident in child and family work, a point made in our research, is confirmed by a comparison of Tables 5.1 and 5.2. Nowhere, for example, in that month's advertisements, is there a post for work with a specific category of elderly person, such as those suffering from senile dementia. (One solitary example, however, appears in the next month's issue, where Essex Social Services Department advertises for 'a specialist for the elderly covering liaison between agencies, review system in some homes, allocation and evaluation of Day Care Unit plus a small caseload of psycho-geriatric people and their families'.)

Although I have heard informally of such experiments, an exciting possibility of work which is both generic and specialised does not appear in the advertisements analysed. The growth of 'fostering and adoption officers' raises the possibility of units or specialist teams for the provision of substitute care across various client groups. The interplay between workers, possibly with different experience, seeking to compare and contrast the needs of different clients for family life, could be enriching and contribute substantially to our knowledge and skill in this field.

It is hard to see how we can escape in general in our organisation of service from the broad client groupings, now so deeply entrenched in social service provision and in the linkages which are required with other professionals. This does not, however, preclude certain experiments such as that suggested above. Nor does it preclude variations on the theme. It is especially important to offer constructive alternatives to the confused, even hypocritical arrangements, which disguise the fact that 'children and family' work frequently excludes a substantial number of children who are physically or mentally handicapped and the fact that ill and elderly clients so often do not receive the family-focused social work service they require. It is interesting that Cooper and Wedge (1980) include physically and mentally handicapped children in their five sub-groups of work with children and families. One or two advertisements in February 1979 give a hint of the flexibility one would like to see. Brent Social Services Department advertised for 'a family caseworker/mental health' in a team 'developing specialist involvement in complex family situations and casework with the mentally disordered'. Wandsworth Social Services Department advertised two posts for social work with 'school children and their families', one for children with 'physical and emotional problems, based at a clinic/health centre', the second for 'service to two units for partially-hearing children'.

The issue which confronts managers of social services departments, however, is how to reconcile creative patterns of specialisation which should probably be based on client groupings with other considerations such as patch work and the differential use of skills. (The last point is discussed at the end of this chapter.)

(C) SPECIAL INTERESTS OF WORKERS

The fifth and last of the factors which have been separated for purposes of discussion concerns the development of informational specialisation or 'concentrations of interest' as the Seebohm Committee described them. These do not seem to have raised objections in principle from any quarter and have been widely accepted as necessary and desirable. Many of the advertisements for generic posts make it clear that these concentrations of interest will be permitted or encouraged, and a number of the respondents in our study gave examples of special interests (although, as mentioned before, these were mostly in the 'child and family' sub-group).

There can be no doubt that it is in the interests of the development of the profession and for the benefit of clients that individual social workers should be encouraged to acquire greater knowledge and skill in areas of work which fire their imagination. It is a step on the road to the creation of expertise within social services departments which, it has been argued, is crucial to their functioning. The proviso is usually made, however, that such interests cannot be allowed to detract from basic 'generic' work and it is acknowledged that the team leader has to be alert to the implications for the work of the team as a whole, especially as social workers move on and a replacement for 'a special interest' cannot be guaranteed. It seems, therefore, that welcome as these interests are, they cannot be a substitute for some formalisation of specialist posts defined as central to team functioning. The emphasis placed by some practitioners on such informal arrangements will not guarantee the availability within the social services department of knowledge and skill of sufficiently high quality, nor of the structures necessary to stimulate and facilitate interprofessional co-operation.

(D) SKILL DEVELOPMENT

So far little has been said about specialisation by the conventional methods of 'casework, groupwork and community work'. It has not been included in the discussion of formal specialisms because, in my opinion, it leads social work up a blind alley. It is apparent that, despite some quite energetic efforts by social work educators, casework, variously defined, remains the method used by the overwhelming majority of social workers. It is difficult to see how it could be otherwise, given 'the caseload' which is at present central to the social work task in an area team. In any case, the divisions increasingly appear artificial for locally based practice. The unitary approach has clearly fired the imagination of some workers, especially if related to some form of patch system. It may be that this is a more constructive way forward and it does not preclude certain workers from developing special interests in certain modes of working, for example, family groupwork, groupwork or behavioural programmes of intervention. To foster such developments, however, consultant advice, even supervision, will be necessary. Enthusiastic social workers need the benefit of stimulation and guidance. The work of Hutchings (1980), a psychologist in a child guidance clinic in Wales, in planning with social workers behavioural programmes in cases of child abuse, affords an excellent example. But this kind of purposeful interprofessional work is rarely available outside London.

Sainsbury (1980, p. 62) gives a preview of his research of 1975–7 concerning the 'content of long term family casework as perceived by social workers and their clients', relating it to the question of specialisation. He compares the work of three agencies, a social services department, a probation department and a family service unit. This is a valuable addition to his earlier work (Sainsbury, 1975), in which client and worker perceptions in a family service unit were minutely studied and from which many fascinating hypotheses were generated.

In the recent research, Sainsbury has collected evidence of nine different kinds of interviewing skills (p. 63), 'the selecting and combining of which in specific case situations represents a major professional expertise'. He argues (p. 64) that

> this complex range of tasks and skills is insufficiently considered when service development is being considered and when, for the sake of convenience, one needs to adopt simplistic definitions of casework practice for example (i) by reference to broad categories of client need . . . and (ii) by an assumption of the existence of 'a method of casework' . . . The fiction of a generic social worker has been developed and maintained by these over-simplifications.

Sainsbury (p. 65) shares my scepticism about the method division:

> If, as I suspect, the so-called methods merely reflect the size of the consumer system to which the worker initially addresses his work, then it is likely that varieties of philosophy, approach and skill transcend the boundaries of the methods and are capable of adaptation and transfer between them.

He suggests (p. 65) that

> specialisation by client group and by method are . . . of limited help. They provide a rough and ready focus . . . and they provide both worker and client with a sense (largely . . . false) of security . . . But these specialisations are not *per se* guarantees of improved service, because of the complexity of task and skill ideally demanded . . .

The broad findings of Sainsbury's research are outlined and include the analysis of reported frequency and perceived helpfulness of certain forms of intervention by both clients and workers and between the two agencies. For example, in local authority work (and also in probation) there is congruence *both* between worker and client *and* between frequency and helpfulness of the use of 'encouragement', which is ranked first out of seven heads. There is a striking dis-congruence between worker and client over 'financial help, which is ranked third by clients both in frequency and helpfulness and seventh and fifth respectively by workers.

This work, set beside the earlier work of Goldberg and Warburton (1979) in 'Seatown', provides some of the much-needed evidence as to how clients view social workers' help. The results are by no means uniformly discouraging, a point of which social workers should take hold, given their tendency only to hear negative findings. Sainsbury uses the material to look at what social workers do well and do badly and from this to consider possible areas of skill development needed to improve the service offered. The general finding (p. 71) is that 'social workers are at their most effective in those problems of family functioning associated with the dynamics of inter-generational relationships and loss of self-regard'. I assume that the cases analysed do not include the elderly or handicapped and that once again 'long-term family casework' has been defined as 'families with children'. However, Sainsbury's finding suggests that there might be fairly easy transferability of these skills to other client groups, if the structures were created to give it impetus. The implications of that statement for social work with the elderly, for example, are very considerable.

Social workers (p. 71) are

> seldom significantly effective (save with children) in problems of role performance not directly associated with interpersonal relationships; for example, work problems, problems of poverty and social deprivation of all kinds, problems of social isolation and social under-achievement.

Sainsbury also suggests (p. 73) that

> sensitivity to specific problems affected the extent to which workers displayed competence in enlisting the help of other services.

It is not possible to do justice to all the issues raised in this brief article. But its conclusions are important in any consideration of specialist skill development. So far as family casework is concerned (and this in itself places certain restrictions upon the findings), Sainsbury suggests that certain skills need particularly to be developed.

(1) 'Welfare benefits advice, combined with effective contact with other major services'. This will come as no surprise; the need is even greater when one recalls the large numbers of short-term clients whom Sainsbury does not include in his study but who take up a high proportion of social work time. However, it is not self-evident that this area of expertise should necessarily be associated with that of social work, or, indeed, that it should necessarily be located within social services departments, a point to which I shall return in the next chapter. Sainsbury does not raise this; in relation to the families he studied the integration of welfare rights advice with other elements of help would be particularly important. These were not 'one-off' clients.

(2) 'Helping people into employment'. This is an issue with which I have been concerned since the period between 1968 and 1970 which I spent as Social Work Adviser to the Supplementary Benefits Comission. Contact with employment officials is a striking omission from Parker's diagram (adapted on p. 80) of interprofessional and organisational contacts which social workers must make. Sainsbury (1980,

p. 72) notes that the probation service was more effective in this area of activity than the local authority workers, which emphasises the influence of 'traditional preoccupations of the services'.

Two research projects between 1970 and 1974 which I directed took place at a time of generally high employment when there was concern about the so-called 'voluntarily unemployed'. In the first, the findings (Hill *et al.*, 1973) demonstrated that this group comprised mainly those in ill-health, of low skill and at the age at which manual labour becomes more difficult. In a further 'in-depth' study (Hill and Stevenson, 1976), the circumstances of some, as perceived by themselves, were analysed. The picture was in general one of difficult family circumstances, past and present, of physical and mental disability or handicap, of economic hardship and of a lack of social skills. Very few of these men had sustained contact with local authority social workers, yet many presented problems in addition to unemployment which, had they been referred, would have been recognised as relevant to the agency. The action research referred to in Chapter 3 in which social workers worked in supplementary benefits offices, confirmed strongly the impression that there had been relatively little social work involvement with the world of work outside the probation service.

This was the case in happier times; a residual group were little helped in this dimension of their living. The present situation changes what is needed from social workers but the sheer volume of the problem may give the issue greater prominence than previously. Social workers will be needed to help men and women and young people with the traumatic social and psychological effects of unemployment and with their practical implications; with realistic plans for re-employment or unemployment and for the constructive use of leisure. Such work, and related family problems, may well be central to the activity of some area teams. Social work has to catch up fast on a neglected area of knowledge and skill. Whether it should remain on the level of an informal specialisation will vary according to local circumstances; and according to whether social service teams should seek to include specialists who are not social workers (see Chapter 6).

(3) 'The development of informal support networks and voluntary help for clients already on their caseloads'. This will be welcomed by those, inside and outside social work, who see this as a way of stimulating local community care. It has been discussed in relation to the patch system in Chapter 3. Sainsbury's finding confirms that of Holme and Maizells (1978), whose national survey revealed a striking difference in the extent to which volunteers were used by local authority social workers and by those in the probation service. However, the authors have some cautionary words which do not necessarily support the implication of Sainsbury's comment – that this is primarily an issue for skill development. Holme and Maizells (1978, p. 182) state:

> The findings of the present inquiry do not support the view that the number of volunteers could be significantly increased in the immediate future if there were 'changes in fundamental attitudes' (Darvill, 1975) or if social workers were trained in new skills. On the contrary, the evidence suggests that if there are limiting factors then these derive less from attitudes or lack of skills . . . than from the effect of the present system of the organisation and management of social services on the practice of social work.

The authors draw attention to three problems. First, the constraints of accountability; secondly, a lack of clarity concerning the place of the voluntary worker which is in turn related to lack of clarity about the social work task; thirdly, they suggest (p. 182) that 'the use of volunteers is more influenced by the untrained than the trained'. This last point is perhaps a little misleading and will vary greatly between authorities according to their percentage of trained staff. However, it remains broadly true that many of the client groups (above all the elderly) who are considered especially suitable for the use of volunteers are served by unqualified, less experienced social workers or by social work assistants. Thus even increased emphasis during training on the development of this skill is unlikely to bear fruit without structural change.

Holme and Maizells (p. 183) quote Bruce who, writing in June 1976 (Volunteer Centre, 1976), cautioned against 'any undue pressure by the statutory services to turn to volunteers only because of the shortages of staff and other resources as a result of present economic difficulties'. It is clear that such warnings will have much greater signficance in the 1980s. The credibility of the profession and the respect with which it is viewed by those in authority will be much affected by the way the profession approaches the use of volunteers in these times of economic constraint. On the one hand, there is undoubtedly a case for more innovative and creative use of voluntary activity, in particular a break with the past associations with middle-class leisure activity and a search for the right way to mobilise working-class altruism. On the other hand, the use of such initiatives to play down the importance of the professional input – in terms of role and skill – is to be deplored. Social workers must continue to develop and to demonstrate their expertise and stake a rightful claim for recognition, which should not (as would be all too easy) be confused with 'job protection' in hard times. If, however, one accepts the analysis of Holme and Maizells it seems that the impetus for more effective use of volunteers must be shared between management and team members. If the latter 'go it alone' the difficulties outlined above are bound to manifest themselves, and may do so in ways which tragically rebound yet again on practitioners; for example, if a child or an old person dies in regrettable circumstances when a volunteer has been visiting, and his or her role and the structure of accountability have been inadequately clarified, this will raise questions concerning professional delegation.

(4) 'Social skills training, combined with the rehearsal with clients of future problematic events in their lives'. There are many dimensions of clients' lives and problems in which such help is likely to be valuable. Perhaps the most topical and striking relates to the help young people may need in presenting themselves for jobs. There are techniques to be learnt in the transmission of such skills and, whilst it may be important on occasion to seek expert help, for example, from psychologists, it is an area in which it seems social

The Organisation of Work (II)

workers could develop much more skill than they have so far. It is a topic to which social work education could make a substantial contribution since it is particularly well suited to the use of audio-visual aids.

Sainsbury would no doubt accept that the four areas discussed are not comprehensive, even within the 'long-term casework' framework, and the intention here is only to illustrate specialisation in terms of skill development. The important thrust of his argument is summed up in the proposal (p. 75) for

> ad hoc specialisation based on task and skill. Central to [its] effective development . . . is the need to discard the notion of a generic worker in favour of a generic team, without which the task/skill dimension of specialisation cannot become fully operative.

The generic team assumes (p. 66)

> a team caseload whereby, although one worker would continue to orchestrate the inputs of work for each case and would provide continuity of experience for clients, all workers would be encouraged to develop personal areas of expertise.

Sainsbury rests his case upon a pattern (p. 67) of 'task allocation and expertise relevant to the personalities available to it' and upon the need to adapt the traditional view of supervision, to provide 'a support and a watchdog'.

These last points, only briefly discussed, are in fact complex. The first is perhaps one of the hardest to work out in practical terms. It necessarily relates to other forms of specialisation discussed earlier which, to use Sainsbury's term, have to be 'orchestrated' if the client is not to receive a fragmented service. I return to this in Chapter 7.

The second point, concerning the utilisation of available talent and interest, is surely the right way to proceed for informal specialisation but reveals 'at a stroke' the need for some formalised arrangements to ensure that basic areas of social work are not neglected.

The third point, which again will be discussed further in

Chapter 7, raises questions concerning the roles of team leaders in any structures which accept the need for formal and informal specialisations of individual team members. In our research report we laid great emphasis on the importance of the team leader in current practice. Any modifications of that practice must include the role of the team leader, its relationship to specialist advisers, and to 'peer relationships' which Sainsbury suggests (p. 67) might offer mutual support in skill development.

In summary, this chapter has considered the structure of teams along various dimensions: first, those which divide work according to its flow and the nature of the problems presented; secondly, those which divide it according to client groups; thirdly, the emergence of posts within teams related to particular needs or opportunities which have been formally defined; fourthly, the case for informal specialism, in particular that associated with the development of skills.

Chapter 6

Boundaries and Connections

Implicit in this book has been the assumption that clients of social workers often need the expertise of others and that their welfare hinges upon a successful interaction between the professionals. In this chapter we explore some difficult 'grey areas', in which the expertise required does not clearly fall within the conventional (some would say reactionary) definitions of social work nor within the traditional remit of some other well-established occupational group or profession such as medicine or teaching. It is not that the boundaries of the other occupations are rigid. On the contrary, their shifts in emphasis and, on occasion, new formulations of elements in their task affect, and are sometimes affected by, social work. The enthusiasm, or lack of it, which one group shows for a particular aspect of the work has a significant bearing on the way boundaries are drawn. For example, the growth in some areas of a cadre of psychiatric community nurses has been encouraged by the lack of impetus from social workers in social services departments for the development of community services for the mentally ill. Again, it may reasonably be presumed that doctors' involvement in social aspects of their patients' welfare is affected by the presence or absence of social workers in hospital. Obviously, however, other factors are at work as well in the way the task is defined. More fundamental changes concerning the nature of the task and the means by which it is to be achieved move other professions nearer to or further away from social work. Perhaps the most striking example of this was the 'therapeutic community' movement, which peaked in the 1960s. The values and assumptions which underlay those developments had much in common with the literature of social work (see Rapoport, 1960). Their regimes laid stress on the understanding and improving of relationships and the development of insight. The treatment programmes were radically changed – fewer drugs and more talk! The blurring of roles between psychiatrists, nurses and social workers which resulted was seen by many as a desirable move away from medical dominance in institutional relationships though Rapoport, amongst others, pointed out the ambivalence, even hypocrisy, that could arise when the chain of command was obscured. Even those most enthusiastic, however, acknowledged the difficulties which arose when there was no clear differentiation of roles within the hospital team.

Another example, though much more powerful in the USA than the UK, is of increased legal involvement in welfare rights. The extent to which this develops and is consolidated will affect considerably the social work task in local authority social services departments.

Thus, there is no set framework within which professions operate; new specialisms arise, created and affected sometimes by powerful ideological commitments, sometimes by important theoretical developments and sometimes as a response to social pressures. This may result in a shift in the demarcation lines; in closer collaborative work, or in higher fences round the boundaries.

The main focus of this chapter, however, is upon aspects of the work of area teams for which, arguably, specialist expertise is needed which is not or has not been clearly seen as integral to social work practice as mirrored in the literature and education. The last section will consider the potential relationship between residential staff and the area team.

The place of social work in social services departments
There have been recurring cries from field workers in social services for clarification of the task, and there has been a considerable confusion between the task of the social services department and that of the social workers within it. It is, of course, obvious that social services departments perform many important functions which no one describes as social work, and some social services directors are irritated by the social workers' failure to realise that, as they say, 'they are small beer'. However, that recognition

has not led to a lively debate on the contribution which occupational groups other than social workers should or could make to social service teams. Nor has the issue been squarely faced – should social work be the pivotal point for all social services activities? The controversy concerning appointments of directors who are not qualified social workers has been a symbol of this confusion. At an earlier stage it was, in my view, politically and professionally essential to assert the independence of social work from medicine. Those medical officers of health who assumed that they would be the first directors of social services had no grounds for assuming their qualifications for such a post were better than or even as good as those of qualified and experienced social workers. But it has become apparent that administrative and managerial expertise is not a necessary component of social work expertise. The span of functions in a social services department casts doubt on the assumption that social work is the only relevant qualification for the post – a point which the present government has implicitly accepted by stating that it will no longer intervene in the appointments of directors who are not social workers. One may question the motives for this – is it part of a destructive cynicism about social work? But it is, in my view, hard to sustain an argument that the appointment of 'a social work director' is integral to the model of a social services department. The only way to defend it is from the somewhat elusive ground of the values which should underpin all the activities of a social services department. Elusive though it may be, this is of crucial importance. There are certain principles which should guide all the policies of a department committed to personal social service. It would, however, be arrogant to suggest that these are the prerogative of social workers, though it may reasonably be asserted that a qualified social worker *should* seek to uphold these principles, which are related to the significance and uniqueness of individual need and the rights of individuals to sensitive service attuned to those needs.

If we were starting again, therefore, and were free of the burden of the pre-Seebohm 'luggage' and of the constraints of earlier structures, it would be profitable to examine the place of other occupational groups throughout the hierarchy, including the area team. There are many who could contribute: teachers *qua* teachers (not as unqualified social workers); lawyers; youth workers; health visitors; geriatricians – all these and many others, as well as the familiar 'OTs' could contribute as full or part-time members of an area team. However, given present economic constraints and the background to the present situation, all one can do at this time is to point out the potentialities of an interprofessional area team and to suggest that, according to local need, there are possibilities for the incorporation into the team of others of equal status, that is, not deemed ancillary or assistant to social workers. A relevant example might be of an executive from industry whose experience of the world of work and of employment and unemployment might be invaluable. Unfortunately, at a time at which such flexibility might have become acceptable, a new anxiety, that of job protection, may become apparent. (What if the choice is *between,* not *as well*?)

The logic of accepting that, for the time being, area teams will in the main be composed of social workers and assistants, using, increasingly, indigenous workers and volunteers, is that even greater concern should be shown to foster interprofessional co-operation in other ways. But there remains the vexed and debated question – what is appropriate work for the qualified social worker?

Social work in relation to help and advice on material problems

The available research, including our own and that of Goldberg and Warburton (1979), shows that a great deal of social workers' time is taken up in giving advice and in mobilising resources. In our study social workers seemed resentful of the time such work consumed. Goldberg and Warburton (p. 124) also comment that although the clients in general were well satisfied with these forms of help 'the social workers often felt frustrated that they were only able to offer practical service and advice'.

An important question which precedes consideration of the role of social workers in such activity is whether such service is, and should be, integral to a statutory personal social services agency or whether it reflects adversely on other agencies who are failing adequately to serve their own clientele or, indeed, on the functioning of our society generally. For example, our research suggested that in some areas (but by no means all) social workers believed that supplementary benefits officials were 'palming off' their customers on social services departments. We cannot assess the validity of such assertions and it is easy for a mythology to build up on such matters. That there has been some confusion of roles is illustrated by Hill and Laing (1979). However, the policy of centralisation of social security offices, with consequent reduction in numbers of local supplementary benefit offices, is bound to increase the demands on social services area staff who are conveniently situated for financial advice or assistance. Indeed, we have heard of some area offices in which callers have asked to ring the more distant offices of the social security, thus avoiding expense of both telephone calls and bus journeys. Rather than frowning upon this, we should perhaps consider the ways in which such a service to the public could be rationalised.

The relationship with supplementary benefits, even with social security more generally, is, however, only one aspect of a wider problem – the extent to which social services departments should act as a link point to a range of agencies connected with their clients' material and financial well-being.

I would argue that an individualised system of social welfare, whose distinguishing feature is that it was created to deal with the unique and diverse problems of individuals and families, must perform an important function in advising clients and negotiating on their behalf. Meyer (1970) has suggested that this need arises from complex and rapidly changing social networks, which the individual cannot find his way round and through by himself. However we may strive to simplify and improve, so that the ordinary citizen can 'work the system' himself, there is no prospect of such an ideal being realised in the foreseeable future. The argument is whether the social services departments should perform these intermediary tasks and whether social workers are the right people to undertake the role. On the first point, it would be wrong to suggest that social services departments are the only significant providers. Citizens' Advice Bureaux and family advice centres, for example, offer alternative ways of meeting the need. Nor do we know how many other agencies serving other purposes, also advise, re-route and perhaps even intervene on behalf of clients who come to the wrong place. Yet it seems likely that an 'unanticipated consequence' of the creation of social services departments has been to provide a wide but vague focus, 'the welfare', to which people naturally come as a first or early port of call. This is strengthened by the greater accessibility which is advocated by proponents of the patch.

Currie and Parrott (1980, p. 14) analyse the flow of referrals following the movement of a team to a more accessible office. They show that office visits increased dramatically in the three months following the move but that the rise

> could not be accounted for in problems connected with housing or financial difficulties . . . The difficulties reached right across the range of areas normally considered appropriate for social work intervention, with emotional and relationship problems being as important as practical difficulties.

They further show that 'in spite of a 32% rise in the number of referrals, the number . . . which required ongoing work actually fell slightly'. (This is slightly puzzling in that one would have expected emotional and relationship problems to have more often required ongoing work.) Be that as it may, common sense suggests that if offices are accessible, clients will drop in more and use them as a first port of call for advice unless they are deterred by psychological barriers! It would seem, therefore, that the social services department must accept this dimension of its activity as a necessary and valuable contribution to welfare.

Related to this is the role of social services departments in 'safety net' financial provision. The arguments and evidence concerning the interface between supplementary benefits and social services departments have been extensively discussed by the present author, and others, elsewhere (Heywood and Allen, 1971; Stevenson, 1973; Jordan, 1974; Hill and Laing, 1979; Valencia and Jackson, 1979). Whatever the important theoretical arguments concerning the proper relation of the supplementary benefits scheme to social work provision, the shape of things to come is fairly clear. The DHSS has decided upon a policy of simplification of the scheme which involves considerable reduction in the use of discretion (DHSS, 1979). The social services departments have certain powers to dispense monies (Children and Young Persons Act 1963, Section I) and to provide material benefits in the form of aids and adaptations (Chronically Sick and Disabled Persons Act 1970). These powers have hitherto been exercised sparingly; shortage of resources is only part of the explanation. There has been considerable reluctance on the part of local authorities and social workers to become involved in the dispensing of money and uncertainty as to how to ration a potentially expensive provision for the disabled population. In the present climate the restraints on expenditure will be even more marked, at the same time as the supplementary benefits scheme becomes, as a matter of policy, less responsive to individual need.

The stage seems set, therefore, for an increase of tension between officials and social workers, although reference is made to the appointment of specialist officers within the social security scheme to ease the problems of certain clients (DHSS, 1979). It is not clear how far the role of such officials will differ from those of special welfare officers, a question which was discussed by the present author in some detail elsewhere (Stevenson, 1973). Nor would their impact be great without a substantial increase in numbers.

Putting these matters together, and adding to them the increase in unemployment with its associated problems, the picture of the social services department of the 1980s which begins to emerge is one in which an even larger proportion of staff time will be devoted not only to advice, brokerage and advocacy, but to finding ways and means, either from within or outside the organisation, of meeting the financial and material problems of clients, including the new 'fuel poverty', with major implications for contact with public utilities. This aspect of social service includes, but goes considerably beyond, the meaning usually put upon the term 'welfare rights'.

If these assumptions prove correct, then the organisation of this aspect of the work will be of crucial significance, both because of its absolute importance and because of the detrimental effect its demands may have upon other equally important areas of service.

What is the case for and against this work being undertaken by qualified social workers? Much of the discussion has been about levels rather than kinds of skill. The question 'do you need a qualified social worker?' carries with it an implication that the work may well not require as much skill. This needs further examination. The characteristics of the work are that it is usually episodic and/or short term; that it will frequently involve contact, by telephone at least, with other officials or professionals. It will range from giving simple straightforward advice which can be proffered by a well-trained receptionist to dealing with immensely complex financial tangles, involving, for instance, debts to private landlords and hire purchase companies, as well as the familiar 'social security' confusions. The problem will sometimes, but by no means always, be associated with problems of a different kind.

Goldberg and Warburton support the argument that social workers need not undertake much of the work they presently accept. They stress the need for 'an effective information and advice service' (1979, p. 126), pointing out that 'it could be manned by information officers with specialised training or it could involve joint arrangements with voluntary bodies'. It is likely that the volume and complexity of the information required to carry out the work would lead in time to a demand for a new form of professional training, possibly with a socio-legal bias. In the meantime it would be feasible for much of the work to be controlled and complex cases handled by graduates or those of equal ability, with some preference for those whose qualifications in social science have given them some valuable background knowledge. They would need in-service training in what might be broadly described as citizens' rights, skills of interviewing and the necessary minimum skills in assessment to judge when referral to a social worker was necessary. This last point is not easily resolved. In the reaction against 'going behind the presenting problem', it must not be forgotten that clients with serious family problems, especially child abuse, do sometimes present at the office with apparently trivial inquiries.

The discussion here has been focused upon the need to make skills complementary to that of social work available within area teams. There is another debate, not taken up here, concerning levels of skill. There is no doubt that some of the tasks assigned to social workers could be undertaken by others less qualified. In my view, however, it is a mistake to relegate information and advice services as such to a lower level and it is for this reason that the notion of a core of graduate personnel is introduced. This is not to deny that there are stupid graduates and intelligent non-graduates! But, on balance, it would seem valuable to introduce into area teams a group of well-educated workers who would not necessarily see this work as leading to social work. (If their careers were not to be blocked, however, the status of an administrative role in local government, equivalent to that in central government, would have to be accepted.)

Community work and social work

Another important boundary or connection has been that between community work and social work. As Sainsbury (1980, pp. 64–5) notes, there has been

> a powerful movement amongst community workers to separate themselves ideologically and professionally from social workers. But within each method, there may now be found a variety of philosophies and a resultant variety of assumptions . . . It is doubtful whether 'method' can be regarded as an appropriate word . . . Specialisation . . . by 'method' of social intervention misses the point that, within [it], the specialist may decide to exercise a broad and complex range of skills and tasks, some of which may lie beyond his personal competence.'

This contentious statement is one with which I have much sympathy, and it is possible that the fierce arguments about the relationship between community work and social work which raged in the 1960s and 1970s will seem dated and irrelevant if some of the ideas discussed earlier, concerning the application of the unitary approach to work in area teams, are taken further by practitioners. That will not mean, however, that the arguments were without value, for the re-emergence of community work, influenced by the political thrust of the left in the early 1960s and the rise of sociology, played an important part in reawakening in social work an awareness of the social and economic determinants of inequality. The tensions which were generated are healthy and necessary in open intellectual and professional systems. It is too early to say to what extent aspects of community work ideology and activity will be incorporated into the ordinary workings of area teams, facilitated by the unitary approach. Incorporation, leading to absorption and, some would say, distortion, is, of course, for some not a desirable goal. It is a Marxist nightmare; the British establishment drains the life-blood from the idea and leaves the corpse masquerading as a living entity. (That there is reality in the fear is readily seen in the ritualistic and empty deference which is sometimes paid to community participation.) But for most of us, most of the time, a philosophy of gradualism is preferred, and this would lead us to search for ways of incorporating valuable elements of new or newly formulated ideas into an existing system. The unitary approach may offer a way of utilising community work which is more effective than the attempt to place specialists within area teams dominated by 'caseworkers'. Our research showed the discomfort experienced by the handful of such workers whom we found in the thirty-one area teams studied. The tensions which we found were confirmed by Thomas and Warburton (1977). They examined the characteristics and attitudes of eleven community workers in 'Exshire'. From what is admittedly a very small survey, they none the less extract valuable points for consideration, including a comparison between the so-called 'endogenous' workers, who had come to community work via casework, and the 'exogenous' who had entered it, and social services departments, by other routes. The former, they found (p. 11) 'seemed able better to manage the simultaneous roles of colleague and internal change agent . . . and that of external change agent in the community'. Certainly, as they present it, the endogenous workers would be much more likely to influence internal systems whilst no less likely to be involved in neighbourhood work. There seems little point in having community workers *in* area teams but not *of* them and it may be that those who see the need to confront bureaucracy must do so from the outside.

In the present economic climate, and with the curious political alliance between left and right which stresses the value of stimulating community networks, it is likely that for community workers whose focus has been on the microcosm of neighbourhood there will be a warmer welcome in social service teams than has so far been the case. However, for a number of vocal community workers, this is patch work in another sense, that of putting a plaster over the wider economic and social injustice which is to be found in deprived areas. Certainly, this is forcefully argued by some of the community development project (CDP) workers (Coventry CDP, 1975; Batley and Edwards, 1978). It is hard to see how their perspective can be translated into action within area teams or social services departments generally. There is little chance of public funds being available to tackle wider structural aspects of deprivation, unless public concern over such issues as unemployment or racial unrest necessitate political action on a wider scale than presently seems likely. But there is much to be gained for the future in some concentration upon the 'micro' rather than the 'macro' systems. Social work can be enriched in both knowledge and skill by studying the outcomes of intervention designed to foster greater social interdependence in very practical ways at local level.

Social work and 'residential work'
I turn now to one of the most crucial boundaries and connections in social work today – that of 'residential work'.

Bucher and Strauss (1961) point out that many professions have developed what might be described as a corporate occupational 'identity' after an earlier phase of separate activity, or even of alliance with others. (The standard example is that of the barber and surgeon who in earlier times put up the same sign. The surgeons' subsequent association with physicians is even now not without its tensions.) The most significant example of such a movement in social work concerns the position of those who provide residential care. Their position, now and in the future, is central to the issues raised in this book about specialisation.

The history of the association between field social work and residential care is complex and has yet to be adequately documented. It is outside the scope of this book to trace it in detail but some points of particular interest and relevance may be noted. First, unlike so many of the issues discussed in this book, the initiative for this association owes little or nothing to the USA. It would seem to be a genuinely British product.

Secondly, there are some analogies with the struggle in field social work to separate itself from medical association. The profession of nursing has played a significant role in the development of residential care. In the early 1950s, to be under 5 and in care seemed remarkably like an illness. Residential nurseries were staffed, from 'Matron' downwards, with nurses in uniform. Although this was challenged in the field of child care, nurses have continued until the present time to be appointed to posts outside hospital, in the residential care of the mentally handicapped and ill and the elderly. Recently, their role in the care of the mentally handicapped has been challenged in much the same terms as for children in care – namely, that there is no inherent, indispensable nursing component in the task which makes a nurse, *ipso facto,* more suitable than anyone else to do the job (Jay Report, 1979). The Jay Committee recommended that there should be a common training for residential staff who work with the mentally handicapped, whether they are employed in the health service, local authority service, or the voluntary sector. This, they recommend (para 241), should be provided under the auspices of CCETSW. However (para 245), the qualification proposed was that leading to the Certificate in Social Service, not the Certificate of Qualification in Social Work. The government reply was given in a parliamentary answer on 22 July 1980:

> The Committee's philosophy and model of care for mental handicap services envisaged a radical change from the present pattern of services to one based on smaller and more local residential units in the community. While welcoming their approach, we have to accept that this shift will be gradual and will take longer than the Committee had hoped, particularly in view of current necessary restraints on public expenditure. We also take the view that the most severely and multiply handicapped people will always need some form of NHS care and more experience is needed on whether this can be provided within the Committee's model of care. In these circumstances whilst we accept the principles underlying the Committee's recommendations we believe it would not be right to urge immediate fundamental changes to the present training arrangements. This is not, in our view, the time to abandon a well tried form of training for nurses – who will continue to provide the majority of mental handicap care staff for some time to come – for one which is comparatively new, and vigorously opposed by nurses and major voluntary organisations. However, we concur with the Committee that the training needs of NHS and social services staff have much in common and that progress should be made in the direction suggested by the Committee. We are therefore inviting the General Nursing Council and the Central Council for Education and Training in Social Work to set up a Working Group to look urgently at ways of introducing common elements within the separate forms of training and providing advice to authorities on the development of common in-service training courses and to come back with a plan for achieving this. This should take account also of the training needs of voluntary organisations. At the same time, we are asking them to consider the feasibility in the long term of a joint training which would lead to a joint qualification for those wanting it.

This somewhat bland compromise is likely to prove difficult to implement and it hides a vigorous battle behind the scenes. Some nurses strongly resisted the loss of this domain and it coincided with a period when neither the government nor the general public was sympathetic to social work. The decision was tartly attacked in a *Guardian* leader (23 July 1980): 'The Jay report on the care of the mentally handicapped was quietly buried yesterday.' The leader argued that 'more could and should have been done' despite the difficulties 'in switching staff training away from the present medical model towards the social skills that residential care workers need'.

It is too early to say whether the suggested compromise will result in the movement desired by many. In any case, it is but one facet of the continuing debate about the desirable balance between nursing and social skills in residential care. Moreover, the recommendation of Certificate in Social Service (CSS) rather than Certificate of Qualification in Social Work (CQSW) further blurred an already confused situation. There is a similar problem in relation to the elderly. Traditionally, the appropriate qualification for residential care of the elderly was seen to be that of nursing. There has been a movement away from this, with arguments advanced which are similar to those concerning the mentally handicapped. The present situation, however, is confused by the fact that increasing numbers of the frail elderly are admitted to homes rather than to hospitals. This may increase rather than diminish the need for some basic nursing skills and knowledge of health care, which are reassuring to the elderly. (However, this does not necessarily imply that a nurse should be 'officer in charge'.)

Thus it can be seen that an occupational group within nursing has emerged in relation to residential care which has been seen to contain a strong element similar or identical to social work. (This is to an extent paralleled between health visiting and field social work.) However, mobility between the two groups is restricted because of the way employment is structured between hospital and local authority work. A nurse, for example, cannot be employed *qua* nurse in the local authority service. Such constraints affect career pattern and promotion prospects adversely.

Another 'boundary area' in residential care has been between teachers and social workers in special schools, especially community homes with education (CHEs). The status and pay of the teachers has been for many years higher, and ever increasing evidence from the 1950s onwards as to the crucial significance of skilled child care practices for children's and young people's development has not altered this.

Even in those areas in which there have not been competing occupational groups, residential care has a continuing struggle to establish its parity of status and esteem with field social work. Concern about child care spearheaded the movement for more training and from the 1950s onwards forms of training for the residential care of children increased. Younghusband (1978), with commendable frankness, remarks (p. 182) that

> there was little interest in the residential task in the care or control of adults during the 1950s and 1960s . . . it was typical of prevailing attitudes that the Younghusband Report (1959) whose proposals revolutionised the training of field staff, was blind to the training needs of residential staffs . . .

What Younghusband describes as a 'breakthrough' occurred in 1967 when the Williams Committee published its report (Williams Report, 1967). It was a move that, according to Younghusband (1978, p. 183), 'finally brought training for this work within the mainstream of social work'. It concluded, however, that residential care had distinctive characteristics which could make it a professional career in its own right; 'a generic training' for all residential work was the model proposed. In fact this did not result in many separate courses being established, and the succeeding years saw efforts to introduce residential 'streams and options' within social work courses, which should have facilitated better integration in practice between field and residential workers, but there is little evidence that this has been the case. Even the increased impetus given by CCETSW, which, in an important discussion document in 1973, declared that 'residential work is part of social work', has only had limited effect. By 1979 there were only about 6 per cent CQSW holders in residential social work, although this represented a significant increase. The very low proportion of staff holding the same professional qualification as field staff in area teams, of whom by this time more than 60 per cent were so qualified, is obviously a factor in the relationship which can or should exist between the two. However, since 1979, there has been another development of far-reaching importance – the establishment of the Certificate in Social Service (CSS). Fifty-seven per cent of the students so far have been drawn from residential settings (CCETSW, 1980). Even so, by the late 1980s, there may still be 70 per cent unqualified staff overall if CSS output is maintained rather than increased. There is no doubt that CSS has 'taken off' and it has many strengths. This is not the place to discuss these at length, nor the far-reaching implications of the scheme for training in the personal social services. However, it is relevant to draw attention to the trend that seems to be emerging, whereby CSS is seen as the preferred form of training for residential work, and to link this with the uncertainty and ambivalence surrounding its status *vis-à-vis* the CQSW. Sadly, colleague relationships are not fostered by goodwill alone. It is my contention that residential workers have much specialist knowledge and skill to offer field workers. That this is as yet only embryonically developed is in part due to long-standing separation and/or differential status. It will be much affected also by the way the relationship between the two types of qualification is worked out, according to their appropriateness for different types of work in residential care.

With these qualifications in mind, there is none the less a powerful case for reviewing the deployment of senior staff in homes. Theories of family interaction and systems theory all point to the need for an understanding of the individual in his social context and in the dynamic interplay of relationships. Residential care covers a wide spectrum of individuals, of all ages and with widely varying needs. For some, relationships outside the home will be (sadly) largely irrelevant: for others, they will be crucial to their present and future well-being. It seems likely that such people will be served best by a division of labour which ensures that, wherever practicable, the staff they know best, who care for them, have not only contact with but responsibility for the maintenance and improvement of the quality of the relationships that mean most to them. This implies involvement far greater than 'being polite to visitors'; it implies skills in social work with families of all clients, whether they be young, old, or disabled. For many years there has been an unresolved tension between field and residential workers. Although this has been in part related to inequality in pay and status, there have also been fundamental difficulties in the interaction of roles which, in a sense, symbolise the divisions so often experienced by the client. It has been extremely difficult for residential staff to empathise with the relatives outside, so often apparently rejecting of, or antagonistic towards, the resident, without the opportunity to see the position, and the problems, from their point of view. The field social worker, although, we hope, sensitive to the problems of caring for disturbed or difficult residents, has rarely had to cope with the intensity of feeling generated in all concerned by the behaviour of some relatives towards some residents. In short, the stage is set for a re-enactment of clients' family tensions by the workers concerned.

For some years it has been apparent that the boundaries of some residential institutions have been getting less rigid. The development of short-term and day care are of major significance in this; when these are combined with long-term care they change radically the focus of the staff task and offer an opportunity for a different perspective upon the relationship between the resident and his place in the community. Even when such care is provided in a different physical location, it represents a kind of bridge between ideas of care – in particular between surveillance and support within the community and 'total' residential provision.

There are two ways in which the expertise which it is to be hoped will develop in this area of social service provision can interact constructively with that in area teams. The first rests upon a detailed knowledge of certain client groups, in particular behaviour patterns characteristic of certain ages and stages. Although the case made by the Williams Committee (Williams Report, 1967) for a generic view of social work in residential care has much to commend it, for many years to come there will be staff whose working life has mostly been spent with a particular client group. The population of the institution in which they work will not afford any natural opportunity, as has been offered to staff in area teams 'after Seebohm', to gain varied experience. Yet very considerable knowledge and understanding, which would be of great value to field workers struggling to support vulnerable people in their homes, has been locked away in some such institutions. Thus, if a cadre of specialist workers were to be built up along the lines discussed earlier, certain key residential staff might well be considered as a resource, whether in relation to clients with whom they had contact, through, for instance, short-term or day care, or through participation in consultation and review of other cases. There will, of course, be major difficulties in translating such an ideal into reality. These are not only due to the real differences in educational background and perceived and real differences in status already discussed. More subtly, for such exchanges to be profitable, the understanding which many residential staff intuitively possess has to be made explicit and applied to a different context. Residential staff may not find this easy, especially if they have not experienced a common training. None the less, the task is worth attempting in quite practical and simple ways. For example, a case presenting severe management problems – say of an elderly woman suffering from dementia and living with her children – could be discussed between the team leader, the social worker and the head of a local elderly persons' home.

In addition to the knowledge which certain residential staff will possess about client behaviour, they have an important contribution to make to the development of interventive skills. Slowness on the part of field workers to develop group work skills was noted by Parsloe, in our research report. Residential staff must develop group work techniques to survive. It is not an optional extra but a *sine qua non* of their work. These may or may not be beneficial to the residents and it is not suggested that field workers will necessarily wish to utilise all the approaches of their residential colleagues! What is suggested is that an analysis of the skills of intervention required and sometimes demonstrated in a residential situation is potentially a rich mine of insights for field workers. In particular, the ways in which the needs of individuals for one-to-one interaction with staff are balanced with the welfare of the group as a whole have obvious parallels with family group work, so much talked about and so little practised. The rapid growth of plans for intermediate treatment of juvenile delinquents is another area (though only one of many) in which residential workers have skills to lend field workers. Our report discussed at some length the insularity of teams and their seeming reluctance to seek advice outside their own group. If this is a general problem, and one which centres upon certain complex group processes discussed by Parsloe (1981), it is not to be expected that such experiments will flourish easily. All that can be done is to note the conspicuous lack of interaction between field and residential staff as conveyed by the lack of comment of our respondents and to suggest that this is wasteful, as well as harmful to clients.

Nothing has so far been said in this book about specialisation *from* area teams *towards* residential care. This is because it has been assumed that specialisms which emerge in relation to client groupings or particular problems will involve close collaboration at certain points with residential staff. However, the lack of comment from the respondents in our research about residential care (except about its scarcity) leads to little confidence that constructive relationships are being reliably and regularly established. It is clearly essential for these links to be forged generally, not only in specific situations such as when children are in assessment centres. A genuine attempt to utilise the experience of residential workers, linked to the other developments, especially in day care, could play an important part in stimulating communication and cooperation in other aspects of work where it is much needed.

There are other 'boundaries and connections' which could have been explored in this chapter. The intention, however, has been to illustrate the way in which field social work interacts or could interact with other occupational groups and to show the fluidity of the position as each group redefines its tasks. This has been examined first, in relation to the 'information and advice' service which takes up and, it is suggested, will continue to take up a substantial part of social service time; secondly, in relation to community work and the unitary approach; thirdly, in relation to residential work. With regard to the last, it has been suggested, *inter alia,* that we are neglecting an important specialist resource.

Chapter 7

Drawing the Threads Together

This short chapter is an attempt to help the reader get above the trees and see the wood. The complexity of the subject and, in particular, the number of factors which, it has been suggested, have to be taken into account in any effective plan for specialisation in an area team, are hard to hold in the mind together. Yet the process of analysis is useless if some synthesis cannot be attempted afterwards. *There can be no blueprint or model which is generally applicable. Demographic characteristics, organisational and professional constraints and personal idiosyncrasies have to be taken into account. The diagram shown offers one suggestion and is, in any case, capable of considerable variation.* It embodies eleven key assumptions:

(1) that a degree of formal social work specialisation is necessary in area teams;
(2) that this does not preclude informal social work specialisation;
(3) that some formal specialisation should be related to broad client groups (but there is room for manoeuvre in the way the groupings are made);
(4) that these groups should link naturally to an essential element in specialisation – interprofessional co-operation;
(5) that there should be a specialist in community needs and resources in every team;
(6) that at least one social worker in each specialist unit should be 'level three', to ensure parity of status, or the worker should have a qualification recognised as of equal relevance and status for the purpose of that area of work;
(7) that social work input be complemented by work of assistants and volunteers and that the possibility of

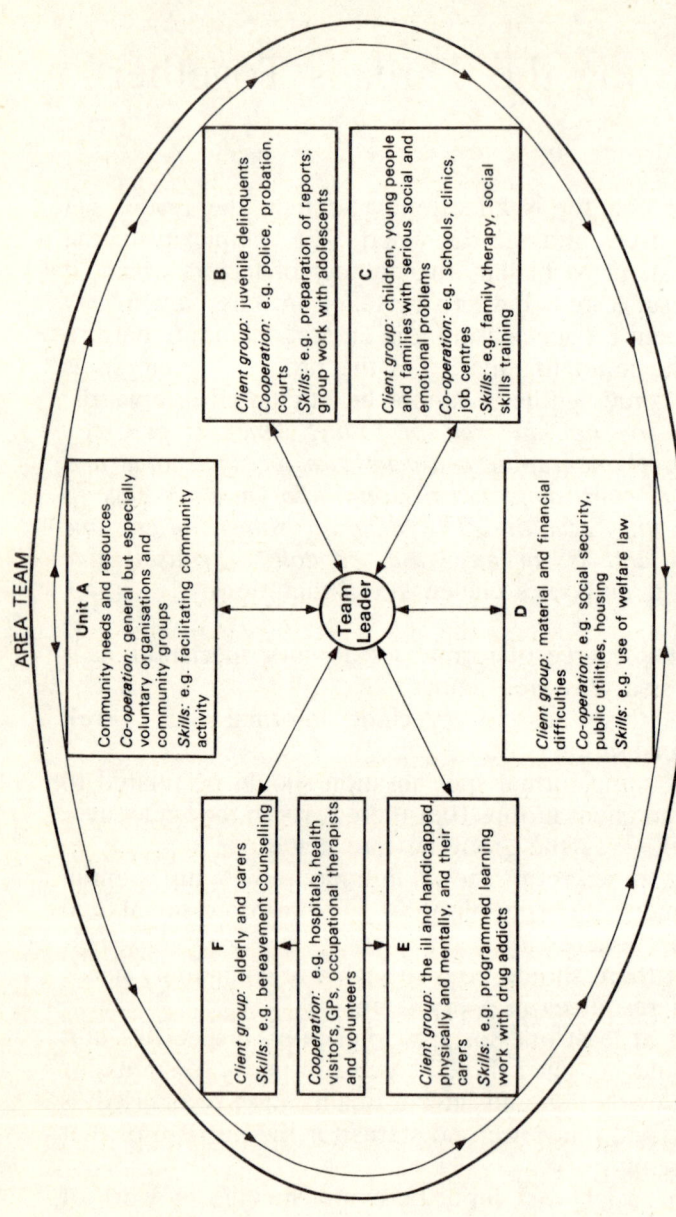

Figure 7.1 One model for team organisation.

NB: (i) Unit D is responsible for duty but uses workers from other units regularly. Unit D takes cases from any client group whose *primary* problems are material and financial.
(ii) In addition to general use of unit A by all units, others will share some cases with key worker in one unit.

Drawing the Threads Together

recruiting other professionals is not ruled out;
(8) that the structure is dependent upon some form of specialist expertise available to the team from outside;

but

(9) that the structure as outlined should be adequate to cope with the large majority of cases;
(10) that not all clients will automatically be assigned to the group designated according to problem or age (allocation should depend on their need of particular service);
(11) that the team leader's role in co-ordination of service within the team is crucial to its effectiveness. This is likely to involve, *inter alia,* regular meetings of the 'level three' workers with the team leader. Such a model places the team leader firmly in the role of manager, whose role in direct staff supervision is less prominent than at present, since experienced and qualified staff would be available to offer this to some workers, leaving the team leader free to offer supervision in areas in which he has particular interest and skill.

It will be seen that the model is of six 'units', dealing with juvenile delinquency and related social and family problems; children, young people and their families with other social and emotional problems; the ill and handicapped and their carers; the elderly and their carers; community needs and resources.

Obviously these overlap and there are other ways of cutting the cake. This way is suggested because of the relatively clear lines it helps to establish between other professional groupings, and because the evidence suggests that, although there will be cases in which the problems require 're-grouping', a large number coming to social services departments at present fall more readily within one category than do some others.

As I attempt to show in the diagram, by the arrowed line round the whole from the 'community needs and resources unit', this unit must feed all the others. The idea is thus to link the strengths of the patch system with the specialist expertise which it is argued is essential also. The linkage of certain skills to the units is *illustrative only*, suggesting, however, that certain skills fall more naturally to be developed in some areas of work. Nevertheless, it is integral to the scheme that the opportunity for such informal specialisation by skill is used generously within the team. Thus, if bereavement counselling is a specialist resource possessed by a social worker with the elderly, it can be shared, through advice, or, on occasion, through short-term direct work, with units coping with other client groups. There is no reason why such expertise should not be effectively used by (say) the social workers dealing with a family in which a child's death was perceived to be central to its disturbance.

In short, it is argued that, if a generically trained social worker in an area team needs to specialise and the notion of 'a generic team' is to be developed, this must not end with a collection of individuals with specialised caseloads who do not share expertise and cross boundaries. *The diagram in practice should show many more lines of contact within the team, in terms of the help they obtain from each other, the contacts they make with other professionals and, on occasion, the sharing of work with individuals or families.* For example, the model could be dysfunctional, and its overall plan defeated, if a worker dealing with a family where abuse of a normal child was the presenting problem, but where there was also a mentally handicapped child, failed to use the knowledge and skill of the relevant worker in assessment and treatment of the family.

In conclusion, some brief consideration needs to be given to the place of social work assistants (or social service officers) in this model. This book has not so far addressed the issue of the role of such workers. This is not to imply that it is insignificant. On the contrary, the success of what has been proposed here would in no small measure depend upon a clarification of their role and upon their availability in sufficient numbers.

Our research (DHSS, 1978, Chapter VI) examined the

position of social work assistants within area teams. It is, I believe, accepted that our findings reflected the position generally in the country, that social work assistants did not assist social workers in the sense of shared case responsibility and that their caseloads were heavily weighted with particular client groups, especially the elderly.

The model proposed here would radically change the way in which such staff are deployed. The numbers needed would vary according to the unit in which they worked, as would their tasks. But all would work directly to a qualified and experienced worker, whether the assistants were designated as social work assistants or social service officers.

Such staff could perform a wide variety of valuable functions, notably in relation to clients with material and financial difficulties and in the mobilisation of community resources. (It is interesting to note that these are two areas specifically mentioned in the CCETSW regulations and guidelines, 1980, p. 53, for the provision of special options on CSS courses.) A further important issue is the redefinition of their established work with the elderly and handicapped. It is likely that the large numbers of the elderly referred to social services departments for relatively straightforward help will make it impossible and inappropriate for initial assessments of all referrals to be made by qualified social workers. However, we have yet to develop training and procedures for routine assessment reports which can be used by social workers to pick out cases requiring more help than apparent in the presenting referral. This is of major importance and is discussed by Rowlings (1981) at some length.

The emergence of schemes for training leading to the Certificate in Social Service cannot be considered in detail here. Suffice it to note that the narrower focus of the training, centering as it does on 'a common unit' and 'standard options', based on client groups and life stages, fits the suggested plan well. Indeed, given the momentum of CSS courses, it is yet another reason why it would be difficult to abandon client groupings in the division of tasks.

It is reported that few schemes have adopted a communities option (CCETSW Paper 9:5, 1980). This is probably due to the lack of structure within which to utilise such skills, which would be provided by models of team service which laid specific emphasis on this sphere of activity. Patch teams are likely to be successful in this respect. The model proposed here, though different, also offers an opportunity to deploy social work assistants or social service officers in specific aspects of community work.

This brief chapter, incorporating in diagrammatic form *one possible* model of the internal functioning of an area team, has deliberately simplified and condensed issues which have been elaborated and debated in the preceding chapters. *Furthermore, it is not intended to foster team insularity, for it assumes the availability of outside expertise.* This has not been presented diagrammatically because so many different patterns for this provision are possible. But in perusing the diagram, the reader is asked mentally to insert arrows inwards to the team – from hospital and residential staff, for example, and perhaps, in some cases, district teams, to indicate that there is knowledge and skill 'out there' to be utilised.

Chapter 8

Some Implications for Education and Training

This chapter explores some of the educational implications of the foregoing discussion. These are far-ranging and complex and would merit a book in themselves. All that can be done, in this concluding chapter, is to ensure that consideration of this key area of specialisation in the development of social work practice within the local authority is not split off from some discussion of one element which is crucial to its success – the provision of education and training.

Although there have been honourable exceptions, the attitudes of employers, managers and social workers in many social services departments have created a climate which at worst is positively anti-intellectual and at best indifferent. In some localities there has been a kind of collusion between these three groups. Employers have needed to be persuaded of the value of education for social workers whereas they might not have questioned it for their teachers; managers have been cost conscious and worried about the logistics of staffing their offices; social workers, nervous of making any claim to expertise which might suggest 'elitism', have not pressed particularly hard for post-qualifying education. These are objectively real problems and do not merely reflect the prejudices of the parties. But their interaction has been unfortunate.

Most local authorities have accepted the objective of qualified field social work staff, although there remains a substantial discrepancy between authorities – differences ranging from 99 per cent qualified to about 25 per cent qualified. In fairness, this contrasts sharply with the battles fought both in children's and health and welfare departments, 'pre-Seebohm', to persuade many employers that basic professional training was relevant. The dramatic increase in CQSW courses between 1960 and the present day demonstrates that much of the employers' resistance was overcome. However, there has remained a quite deeply entrenched view that once this professional qualification has been obtained, further education is an 'optional extra'.

Recently the attitudes of employers and managers have been affected by two factors. First, there was the social workers' strike. Some of those authorities which experienced the worst effects of the strike were those which had worked the hardest to recruit trained workers or to second for training those whom they employed. Whatever the justification for, or explanation of, the action which such social workers took, it was bound to raise questions in the minds of employers concerning the impact of training on their work force. Thus the strike may have reinforced some of the dissatisfaction, never far from the surface, concerning the nature of the training provided for work in local authority social services departments.

The second factor, of major significance, has been the growth of the new model of training leading to the Certificate in Social Service, in which the agency as a whole, and staff at different levels, have played a major part. We have much to learn from the partnership which has evolved between the local authority and the educational institutions and it may in time lead to some radical restructuring of CQSW courses. Meanwhile, however, it tends to strengthen a certain disenchantment with CQSW courses and, dangerously, to overlook, or underplay, the long-term effects on an emerging profession of education tied so closely to an employing body.

As it appears at present, it looks as if many social services departments, within the context of severe constraints, will continue to give priority to CSS development, especially for residential staff; some, but not all, will continue to work towards a higher percentage of CQSW qualified staff; a few will support the post-qualifying schemes which CCETSW has sought to foster, of which there are presently about thirty. My own view is that without advanced skills at the first layer of management and at senior practitioner level, the work done by newly qualified CQSW staff and by CSS holders will lack direction, both organisationally and professionally, and seriously impair the overall quality of service offered.

This does not mean, however, that there is no need for changes in the content and structure of CQSW courses, including fieldwork placements. Furthermore, it would be pessimistic (and unrealistic) if one were not to consider the diverse ways in which in-service training, short courses and machinery for consultation and supervision could be developed to contribute to emerging patterns of specialisation. It is to these I now turn.

Our research (Chapter XIV) gave some cause for concern that CQSW courses might not have been able effectively to grasp the educational nettles of generic practice. In particular, there was some evidence of negative, even hostile, attitudes on the part of those who taught social workers towards the local authority as an organisational context for social work. However, this was probably less serious than the implications of Browne's account (Chapter V) of the difficulties which social workers had in conceptualising or even making explicit the rationale for their work. There are a number of dimensions to this which Parsloe explores (Chapter XIV). As suggested earlier (Chapter 1) practitioners and educators have been slow to develop between them bridging concepts which have clear application to practice in social service departments, or indeed to social work more generally. As was discussed in Chapter 2, some educators struggled to provide 'generic training' before there were appropriate structures to which it could be applied. Yet when the structures were created, the profession was unprepared. With hindsight, it is regrettable that so little consultation took place between courses, that there was so little planning for students between courses and agencies and that there was so little in-service training to prepare workers for their new setting. Fragmentation at central government level, including that of the training councils, was no doubt partly the cause. It is understandable that at such a time of upheaval students should be of low priority, but it has had long-term repercussions in confusion and uncertainty regarding the expectations and objectives of 'a local authority placement'. In short, if the social workers and their managers did not know what they were doing or, and this is more important, what they *should* have been doing, it was hardly to be expected that teachers and students would be able to show the way.

What would follow for student placements from the model of an area team which has been outlined in the previous chapter? It was argued in the first chapter that 'a generic training' should remain the objective of a CQSW course. The consquences of preparing basic grade social workers for specialised work would be to fragment the profession yet again and seriously to reduce staff mobility. However, the model proposed, even if considerably adapted, would offer opportunities for focused work in a number of areas with specialised supervision, which would then have to be put into a framework which sought to clarify the similarities and differences between the kinds of work undertaken. This would be the responsibility of the tutor, practice teacher and student and would be one important focus for supervision, in both dyads and triads.

There follow two hypothetical examples, constructed to show the possibilities of this approach. They relate to the model in the previous chapter but it must be emphasised yet again that it is only one of the possible variations upon the theme.

Example A
The placement is a block of three months.

Miss A is a student in the second year of a two year course. She is a non-graduate, aged 29, with two 'A' levels. She is seconded by the social services department in which she worked as a social work assistant for two years. This work was mainly with the elderly but also involved regular turns 'on duty'. Before that, she had done voluntary work in a club for mentally handicapped children. Her first placement was in a Probation Department, which was much enjoyed and she had had a six-week placement in a children's home which she did not enjoy.

Miss A's nominated supervisor is Mrs B, a level three

Implications for Education and Training

social worker in the children, young people and families section. Formerly a worker in a Family Service Unit, she has had considerable experience in work with so-called 'problem families'. In this team, before moving to her present post, she had worked in the unit dealing with delinquency.

A plan for Miss A is worked out, which takes into account both her previous experience and that of her supervisor. It is agreed that Miss A needs to deepen her knowledge and skill in certain areas rather than spend much time learning about the workings of the team generally.

In her previous work, she was completely 'case-oriented' and had little opportunity to engage in aspects of community activity. It is agreed that, throughout the placement, she will spend a day a week with the community needs and resources section, in which she will assist in giving support and advice to a newly formed group of street wardens. This work will be discussed directly with the worker in charge of that unit.

In her previous work, she had had experience of 'doing duty'. However, it is agreed that she should have a short period of observation at the beginning of the placement to study the way it is organised, which is quite different from the way it operates in her own agency, observe some interviews and discuss the management of this aspect of the team's work with the worker in charge.

Her work with the elderly and the handicapped has given her little opportunity to work in any depth. It is agreed that from the end of the period of observation, she will have a small group of such clients who require fairly intensive work, consequent upon a 'life crisis' – for example, bereavement, the sudden onset of illness or the birth of a handicapped child. If any of these arise spontaneously from the period of observing 'duty' so much the better. She will be supervised directly on these cases by the worker in charge of either of the two units.

The remaining two or three cases requiring systematic, planned work, will be drawn from any of the two groups dealing with the social and emotional problems of families with children and will be supervised by Mrs B. Miss A gained experience of courts and court reports in her first placement so this will not be repeated. She has little experience of problems of unemployment or of contact with schools so cases will be selected if possible to provide an opportunity to make contact with relevant agencies. One of the workers in Mrs B's unit has a particular interest in social skills training, and Miss A is keen to learn about it. So an attempt will be made to utilise this in relation to cases chosen – for example, for an unemployed teenager. In any case, Miss A will sit in on some of the workers' interviews to learn more about it. She did not enjoy her placement in a children's home and is keen to have one case involving plans for a child in residential care to seek to get this in perspective.

The nominated supervisor, Mrs B, is accountable for all Miss A's work to the team leader and professionally responsible to the educational institution. To fulfil these obligations, Mrs B will read all the student's records, including her reports on her work with the 'community unit' and on the observation of duty. She will discuss these with her. At some points a tripartite discussion with the unit worker for the elderly and handicapped will be held to appraise her professional development. Miss A knows her work will be discussed informally with other team members involved, that this will not be formalised unless there are problems but that their observations will be included in her final report.

Example B
The second example is of Mr C, a young graduate in modern languages. He is 24 and has had a year's experience working in a voluntary organisation which provides sheltered housing. He knows little of local authority work and wonders whether, in the longer run, he will want to specialise in some form of community or welfare rights activity. He is on a grant and not committed to work in a social services department, although it is likely that he will begin his career there.

His nominated supervisor, Mr D, is the worker in charge of the juvenile delinquency unit. Mr D has had several years' experience in youth and community work before taking a professional qualification in social work. He has a particular interest in the development of intermediate treatment and has close links with the worker in the 'community section' in connection with this.

Mr C's learning needs are explored and a plan drawn up. It is agreed that he needs to gain some fairly general experience of the workings of the team, partly through discussion and observation, on the understanding that he will then need some more concentrated and specialised experience in his second placement, the nature of which will depend in part on the way his interests develop. His placement spans four months, with block periods at the beginning and end and three days weekly in the spring term.

Mr C will spend two weeks 'doing duty' under the supervision of an experienced worker (not the worker in charge). During this time, he will take everything that comes and a watch will be kept for new cases which must be taken on to meet his other learning needs. During the two weeks, the worker in charge of the unit will set him certain specific 'finding out' tasks in relation to clients' more complex material and financial problems and will discuss these: for example, complicated hire purchase agreements or financial difficulties arising from maintenance agreements. At the end of the block period, Mr C will continue to 'do duty' at certain times, say once a fortnight.

During the ten weeks of 'three-day weeks', the intention will be to give Mr C a wide range of experience which should include the following:

at least two court reports, with associated contact with professionals and attendance at court. This will be supervised by Mr D;

at least two cases concerning the elderly and handicapped, which should not be of a purely practical kind. Emphasis should be placed on the examination of community networks, actual and potential, and links should be encouraged with 'the community unit';

at least two cases concerning severe family problems, including one where a family member is mentally ill since Mr C has expressed a particular anxiety about this. Mr C's formal supervision on these cases will be with Mr D, but some tripartite discussions will be arranged with the worker who has a special interest in mental illness and who may well take the case when Mr C leaves.

In cases involving physical or mental illness opportunities should be taken for Mr C to visit hospitals and to discuss issues with social workers and medical staff, including general practitioners, of which he has little experience.

In the final block period of two weeks Mr C will continue,

where appropriate, with his cases, although the emphasis will be on techniques of closure. He will spend time observing and, where possible, participating in the activities of the 'community unit', to which by then it is to be hoped that he will be well linked in, through his cases and the interests of his supervisor in intermediate treatment.

Mr C's nominated supervisor, Mr D, has the same responsibilities as Mrs B. It is deliberately planned that his supervision should be largely vested in Mr D, whereas in Miss A's case it is split between two workers. This acknowledges that the student's needs are less sophisticated than Miss A's at this stage, and that the gains of careful concentration by one experienced worker upon Mr C's work outweigh Mr D's lack of special expertise in certain areas, provided use is made of other workers' knowledge and skill. Mr D will receive reports on his student's progress from the 'duty' and 'community' units and these will be incorporated in the final report. Both students will join with any others in attending team meetings and in having regular discussions with the team leader concerning his own role and the management of the team as a whole.

It is easy to pick holes in these arrangements, to point out that such experience may not be available and that the best laid plans go awry. The intention has been, however, to show how in practice a student might profit from a generic team, with specialised expertise available, without the experience becoming fragmented in a way which would hinder professional development and mask difficulties. Difficult to convey, but crucial to the success of any such plans, is the flexibility needed by the nominated supervisor in looking for the right people to teach the student the things he needs to know. 'The package' for each student examines critically their past experience so that it is neither replicated nor ignored. For example, it is not enough to say, 'Miss A has worked with the elderly, we will leave that out'; past experiences may be negative, narrow or unimaginative and may need challenging. Similarly, Mr C's interest in 'welfare rights' needs fostering but not to the detriment of other work he will in all probability have to undertake. In particular, fears and anxieties about specific areas of work need to be tackled at this early stage.

Implications for Education and Training

These examples should not reinforce the insularity of teams in their provision of opportunities for students. Any chance that arises spontaneously from situations or cases can be utilised to increase the student's awareness of the resources which exist outside the team for his own learning. Where these do not arise, specific opportunities can be devised. However, some modification of the 'one-to-one' model of supervision is needed if the best use is to be made of available talent and it is here suggested that it is feasible. The merit of such 'packages' is not only that they take sensitive account of the student's needs but that they can offer alternatives which may be equally satisfactory, to allow for the changes in team structure which are unavoidable. There are few students whose range of interests is so narrow that reasonable adjustments to the agreed plan cannot be made.

This says nothing about the way this is integrated with the course curriculum or about the tutors' relationship with the agency. It is not within the focus of this book to discuss the problems of curriculum planning generally but some observations are relevant to the generic/specialist debate.

No two-year course – let alone a one-year course – can provide a systematic grounding in the range of knowledge and skill required to operate competently in all the areas presently defined as the work of an area team immediately after training. In the longer run this must have implications for the desirable length of a CQSW course, but the present economic climate makes that unlikely to be more than a discussion point for some years. In the meanwhile the efficiency of the existing courses in preparing students for work in social services departments can only be judged on the following five criteria.

First, continuing efforts need to be made to develop the bridging concepts referred to in Chapter 1. These are not only concerned with the common ground between clients' needs and problems but also with the transferability of skills. The latter has been moved on by the development of the 'unitary approach' but much depends on the structure of practice in the field,. There are opportunities here for partnership between practice teachers and tutors. Social work theory cannot be taught in a practice vacuum.

So far as the former is concerned, the example of 'loss', given in Chapter 1, only scratches the surface of an important and exciting intellectual challenge. There are many ways in which generic themes can be followed through. For example, if the reception into residential care of children and old people are considered together, vitally important similarities and differences emerge; similarly, if the provision of substitute care were taught generically, it might provide the springboard for some of the experiments discussed in Chapter 5. It is therefore important to avoid the creation of special options or interests which mirror present divisions and positively dissuade students from thinking generically. Teachers are as much at the risk of 'blinkered vision' as anyone else and the temptation simply to accept conventional groupings for teaching purposes is strong, not least because of the professional experience and interests of teachers concerned. It is not suggested that there should be *no* such groupings, simply that we should search for new ways of analysing and classifying the nature of the problems with which social work deals and the models of intervention open to it.

Secondly, of course, the educational institution must take overall responsibility for the planning of programmes for individual students. In so doing, as in the examples given earlier, an effort must be made to strike a sensible balance between breadth and depth and to build on past experience wherever possible, as well as utilising the strengths of the team as a whole.

Thirdly, the responsibility for life which social workers in a social services department carry when qualified places a moral obligation on the educational institution to teach them to be aware of what they do not know. Thus, they cannot, on qualification, 'know' the details of law which some employers seem to require, but they should be 'legally sensitive', so that they are quick to see where they may need to seek advice or exercise caution in their intervention. Similarly, they cannot be immediately expert in cases of child abuse, but they should know enough of the literature on 'predictors' to be alerted to consult the experts when certain cases show particular characteristics.

Fourthly – a more personal view – newly qualified workers should identify interprofessional work as crucial to their task, which has implications for course content.

Fifthly – and more contentious – there should be no assumption, implicit or explicit, conveyed by the course ethos, that some client groupings merit or require more skilled social work than others. Courses may do much, through teaching and placement expertise, to affect this. In particular, teachers of core subjects, such as social policy, sociology and psychology may be encouraged to illustrate their central themes so as to cover, fairly equitably, the people and problems with which social workers are faced. The way such examples are used is as important as the volume of the teaching, which has to be curtailed.

The limitations which, I believe, are inevitable in CQSW training as a preparation for local authority work cannot be remedied by the constant addition of 'more'. Nor do they logically lead to the reintroduction of specialisms, although allowance may be made for special interests. The only way forward is by systematic provision for staff development at post-qualifying level available to all CQSW holders.

The phrase 'staff development' is usefully vague. Much can take place within the agency and within the team but it should be legitimated by management and given appropriate status. (The position of training officers has in many authorities been equivocal, if not unsatisfactory, and has deteriorated recently in the face of cuts.) Furthermore, staff have some responsibility to pursue aspects of professional education in their own time. Such opportunities as the Open University offers have been taken up by many professionals at considerable personal cost. It may be that we have taken educational opportunity too much for granted. However that may be, it would be my contention that employing authorities have an obligation to provide, or facilitate the provision of, educational opportunities for staff development. I would go so far as to say that without this the credibility of social work in the local authority, already at a low ebb, may be irrevocably damaged. Economies, therefore, which strike first at training, are dangerously false.

There are a number of different facets to such staff development. Within the framework discussed in the previous chapter various staff might provide the newly qualified worker with the supervision he needs on specific aspects of his work, provided it was clear to whom he was accountable within the team for his work as a whole. This would usually be the team leader, who would also formally appraise his work. These arrangements could be linked to schemes of accreditation and probationary periods. An induction period of about a year would be desirable. During that period a new worker might gain experience, both in areas of work in which he was lacking and in areas in which he was especially interested. As with students, and following through from that experience, a learning programme could be formulated. (Some social services departments are presently attempting to put this into action.) It implies an element of protection, but the worker, according to his abilities and experiences, could quite quickly build up a workload considerably larger than that of a student. The team leader would not be expected to offer the specialist expertise which some of his colleagues could give. This was one of the vicious circles we found in our research which has somehow to be broken. The team leaders' experience, usually with 'children and families', often made then doubtful of their ability to offer effective supervision 'across the board' to new workers. If a degree of specialisation develops, it can be made available both to students and staff, thus raising the overall quality of social work service to neglected client groups.

At the end of a period of induction, the worker might move into one or two units, depending on his interests and team needs. Different combinations are possible and unless the worker has problems in relation to authority or highly developed specialist interests, bridging of more than one of these would be beneficial to both worker and team. Certain combinations would be easier to manage than others, but none would be impossible. Experience must show how the various transitions are best accomplished – and when – to the benefit of the worker and without detriment to the client. But it is easy to see that a more experienced worker might continue with a few long-term cases in one unit until the appropriate time for closure or transfer, whilst developing skills in a different aspect of practice elsewhere.

Thus, in the first stages of a career after qualification, much could be achieved by carefully planned individual programmes, 'topped up' with departmental workshops or other short courses at appropriate times. It may be that there has been some waste of time and money when workers have flitted to short courses without a clear view of 'why this – now?'

At the stage at which a social worker moves to specialisation at 'level three', some form of longer post-qualifying course seems essential; indeed, it should perhaps be a condition of taking up such a post. At the present time, the appropriate courses are not all available and those that are are under-utilised. Even if they are available and used, however, there is a need for ongoing support and consultation. This might be obtained between teams, and include residential care staff. It would have the secondary benefit of breaking down the insularity of teams.

The expertise available from outside the social services department, however, should also be identified and used. For example, if some geriatricians would agree to discuss certain cases and problems with the social work specialists, the gains might not only be for the social workers about individual cases but may lead to a better understanding of each other's roles. Such arrangements, formally approved by management, would leave specialist advisers, if such were employed, more free to co-ordinate information and advice to their departments both 'up' and 'down' the hierarchy, as well as more able to undertake liaison work with outside professions and institutions in relation to policy issues.

Reference has been made earlier to the role of the team leaders and their significance in any changes in team structure which emphasise specialisation. It should be essential for all team leaders to undertake some formal education and training for their task, which would be more concerned with the deployment and appraisal of staff and the overall management of work than with individual supervision of staff. It would be for the team leader to ensure that the team was in reality 'generic', by the sharing of knowledge and skill and the flexible allocation of work. But in this he should be supported by experienced and well qualified colleagues at 'level three'.

Some of the arrangements would have financial implications, both in terms of staff levels and time, and, on occasion, payment for consultancy. There is then the inevitable cry: 'we cannot afford it.' All that can be said is that, in determining financial priorities, there is no escape from clarification of the value placed upon education and training. Central to my argument throughout this book has been an assumption that social work in area teams is a difficult and demanding task with requires, *inter alia,* intellectual activity of quite a high order. This has to be fed by the available and rapidly growing knowledge of the behavioural and social sciences as well as of interventive skills. Otherwise it will atrophy. If that assumption is accepted, then there will be financial implications for the education of the social workers; in particular, much more attention than has been given previously should be shown to their post-qualifying needs, especially for team leaders. However, following our research, we were not sanguine that the abilities and energies of workers were in general being used as effectively or productively as possible. It may be, therefore, that to reject the costs of systematic staff development is to be penny wise, pound foolish, since it should contribute substantially to clarification of the task of the social worker in the social services department.

From 1973, when CCETSW first asked me to undertake work on specialisation, I have been aware that the issues were of crucial importance to the development of social work in the local authority. The findings of the research project undertaken between 1974 and 1977 served only to reinforce that view. Social services departments are the employers of the vast majority of social workers (including those in hospitals) in this country. The area teams seem likely to remain a focal point for service delivery. However the details are worked out it seems essential to retain two

Implications for Education and Training

elements in such teams, organised in ways that will be mutually enriching and which will take account of staff strengths and weaknesses. First, there is the element of local community service, in which the needs are discovered and resources mobilised; secondly, the element of specialisation which makes available to certain clients particular knowledge and skill in relation to their problems.

In such developments, the third essential ingredient is the utilisation of knowledge and skill outside the team; it seems that there are such resources, not identified at present.

The current economic stringency may hold back certain innovations and, in particular, increased expenditure on staff development. However, one can plan for better times. Furthermore, greater staff stability may give increased incentive to develop patterns of service which are stimulating to staff. Nor should it be assumed that all developments along the lines proposed here are expensive; they rest more on imagination and initiative than upon hard cash.

Bibliography

Auckland Report (1975), *Report of the Committee of Inquiry into the Provision and Co-ordination of Services to the Family of John George Auckland* (London: HMSO).
Ausubel, D. (1958), *Theories and Problems for Child Development* (New York: Grune & Stratton), quoted in Bartlett (1970).
Bartlett, H.M. (1970), *The Common Base of Social Work Practice* (London: National Association of Social Workers).
Batley, R., and Edwards, J. (1978), 'Community development project and the urban programme', in *Action Research in Community Development*, ed. R. Lees and G. Smith (London: Routledge & Kegan Paul), pp. 161–8.
Biestek, F. (1961), *The Casework Relationship* (London: Allen & Unwin).
Bowlby, J. (1969, 1973, 1980), *Attachment and Loss*, Vols I, II and III (London: Hogarth Press).
Browne, E.T. (1979), 'The challenge of work with mentally handicapped persons and their families', monograph, Department of Social Policy and Social Work, University of Keele.
Bucher, R., and Strauss, A. (1961), 'Professions in process', *American Journal of Sociology*, vol. LXVI, no. 4, pp. 325–34.
Butrym, Z. (1976), *The Nature of Social Work* (London: Macmillan).
Bywaters, P. (1978), 'The unitary approach in practice', *Social Work Today*, vol. 9, no. 35, pp. 17–19.
Central Council for Education and Training in Social Work (CCETSW) (1973), 'Residential work is part of social work', Working Party Report (London: CCETSW).
CCETSW (1980), 'CSS progress report', *CCETSW Paper 8:4* (London: CCETSW).
CCETSW, (1980), 'Regulations and guidelines for CSS', *CCETSW Paper 9:5* (London: CCETSW).
Colwell Report (1974), *Report of the Committee of Inquiry into the Care and Supervision provided in relation to Maria Colwell* (London: HMSO).
Cooper, J., and Wedge, P. (1980), 'Children and families: some issues for social work policy and practice', in T. Booth et al (eds) *Specialisation: Issues in the Organisation of Social Work* (London: British Association of Social Workers/Social Services Research Group, pp. 47–61.
Coventry Community Development Project (1975), *Coventry and Hillfields: Prosperity and the Persistence of Inequality* (London: Home Office and City of Coventry with the Institute of Local Government Studies).
Currie, R., and Parrott, B. (1980), 'A unitary approach to social work', unpublished monograph.
Department of Health and Social Security (DHSS), (1978) *Social Service Teams: The Practitioner's View* (London: HMSO).
DHSS (1979 a), 'The reform of the supplementary benefits scheme',

White Paper, Cmnd 7773 (London: HMSO).
DHSS (1979 b), *Review of the Supplementary Benefits Scheme* (London: HMSO).
Dundee University (1975), 'A unitary approach to social work practice' (Dundee: University of Dundee).
Glampson, A. et al. (1975), *A Guide to the Assessment of Community Needs and Resources* (London: National Institute for Social Work).
Godfrey, Lisa, Report (1975), *Report of the Joint Committee of Inquiry into Non-Accidental Injury to Children with Particular Reference to Lisa Godfrey* (presented to the Area Health Authority (Teaching) of Lambeth, Southwark and Lewisham, the Inner London Probation and After Care Committee and the London Borough of Lambeth).
Goldberg, E.M., and Neill, J. (1972), *Social Work in General Practice* (London: Allen & Unwin).
Goldberg, E.M., and Warburton, R. (1979), *Ends and Means in Social Work* (London: Allen & Unwin).
Goldstein, H. (1973), *Social Work: A Unitary Approach* (Columbia, NY: Columbia University Press).
Hadley, R. (1980), 'Social services departments and the community', paper presented to the Policy Studies Institute Seminar.
Hadley, R., and McGrath, M (1979), 'Patch based social services', *Community Care*, 11 October, pp. 16–18.
Hadley, R., and McGrath, M. (1980), *Patch Based Social Services Teams, Bulletin No. 1* (Lancaster: Lancaster University Press).
Hall, A. (1974), *The Point of Entry* (London: Allen & Unwin).
Hallett, C., and Stevenson, O. (1980), *Child Abuse: Aspects of Inter-professional Co-operation* (London: Allen & Unwin).
Halsey, A.H. (1964), 'Government against poverty in school and community', reprinted in M. Bulmer (ed.), *Social Policy Research* (London: Macmillan, 1978) pp. 139–59.
Harlesden Community Work Project (1979), *Community Work and Caring for Children* (London: Owen & Wells).
Heywood, J., and Allen, R. (1971), *Financial Help in Social Work* (Manchester: Manchester University Press).
Hill, M., and Laing, P. (1979), *Social Work and Money* (London: Allen & Unwin).
Hill, M., and Stevenson, O. (1976), 'From the general to the specific', unpublished monograph.
Hill, M. et al. (1973), *Men Out of Work* (Cambridge: Cambridge University Press).
Hollis, F. (1964, 1972), *Casework: A Psycho-social Therapy* (New York: Random House).
Holme, A., and Maizells, J. (1978), *Social Workers and Volunteers* (London: British Association of Social Workers).
Home Office with Ministries of Education and Health and Scottish Home Department (1950), *Circular 157/50* (London: Home Office).
Hunt, A. (1964), 'Enforcements in probation casework', reprinted in Younghusband (1966), pp. 155–66.

Hutchings, J. (1980), 'Behavioural work with families where children are at risk', paper presented at the First World Congress on Behaviour Therapy, Tel Aviv, Israel, July.

Ingleby committee (1960), *Report of the Committee on Children and Young Persons*, Cmnd 1191 (London: HMSO).

Irvine, E. (1952), 'The function and use of relationship between client and psychiatric social worker', reprinted in Younghusband (1966), pp. 88–94.

Jay Report (1979), *Report of the Committee of Inquiry into Mental Handicap, Nursing and Care* (London: HMSO).

Jeans, M. (1979), 'Role analysis in field social work – the development of a new model', Devon Social Services Department.

Jordan, W (1974), *Poor Parents* (London: Routledge & Kegan Paul).

Kane, R. (1975), *Interprofessional teamwork*, Manpower Monograph No. 8 (Syracuse, NY: Syracuse University Press).

Lonsdale, S., Webb, A., and Briggs, T.L. (eds) (1980), *Teamwork in the Personal Social Services* (London: Croom Helm).

Malherbe, M. (1979), 'Accreditation in Social Work' (London: CCETSW).

Marris, P. (1974), *Loss and Change* (London: Routledge & Kegan Paul).

Mattinson, J., and Sinclair, I. (1979), *Mate and Stalemate* (Oxford: Blackwell).

Meyer, C. (1970), *Social Work Practice* (New York: The Free Press).

Meurs, Stephen (1975), *Report of the Review Body appointed to Inquire into the Case of Stephen Meurs* (Norwich: Norfolk County Council).

Moore, W.E. (1964), *Social Change* (Englewood Cliffs, NJ: Prentice-Hall).

Packman, J. (1975), *The Child's Generation* (Oxford: Blackwell).

Parad, H. (1965), *Crisis Intervention* (New York: Family Service Association of America).

Parker, R. (1980), lecture to students at Bristol University, unpublished.

Parkes, C.M. (1972), *Bereavement – studies of grief in adult life* (London: Tavistock).

Parsloe, P. (1981), *Social Services Area Teams* (London: Allen & Unwin).

Peacock, Simon (1978), *Report of the Committee of Inquiry* (Cambridge: Cambridgeshire County Council).

Perlman, H. (1975), *Social Casework: A Problem Solving Process* (Chicago: University of Chicago Press).

Pincus, A., and Minahan, A. (1973), *Social Work Practice: Mode and Method* (Itasca, Ill.: Peacock).

Presthus, R. (1979), *The Organisational Society* (London: Macmillan).

Rapoport, R.N. (1960), *The Community as Doctor* (London: Tavistock).

Reid, W.J., and Epstein, L. (1972), *Task Centred Casework* (Columbia, NY: Columbia University Press).

Reid, W.J., and Shyne, A.W. (1969), *Brief and Extended Casework* (Columbia, NY: Columbia University Press).

Rowbottom, R. et al. (1974), *Social Services Departments* (London: Heinemann).

Rowe, J., and Lambert, L. (1973), *Children Who Wait* (London: Association of British Adoption Societies).

Rowlings, C. (1981), *Social Work with Elderly People* (London: Allen & Unwin).
Sainsbury, E. (1975), *Social Work with Families* (London: Routledge & Kegan Paul).
Sainsbury, E. (1980), 'A professional skills approach to specialisation' in *Specialisation: Issues in the Organisation of Social Work* (London: British Association of Social Workers/Social Services Research Group) pp. 62–76.
Seebohm Report (1968), *Report of the Committee on Local Authority and Allied Personal Social Services* (London: HMSO).
Social Services Study Group (1979), *Social Work and the Systematic Provision of Local Authority Social Services* (London: Association of County Councils/Association of Metropolitan Authorities/Local Authority Conditions of Service Advisory Board/Local Government Training Board).
Specht, H., and Vickery, A. (1977), *Integrating Social Work Methods* (London: Allen & Unwin).
Stevenson, O. (1963), 'Co-ordination reviewed', *Case Conference*, vol. IX, no. 8, reprinted in E. Younghusband (ed.) (1967), *Social Work and Social Values*, (London: Allen & Unwin), pp. 113–20.
Stevenson, O. (1971), 'Knowledge for social work', *British Journal of Social Work*, vol. I, no. 2, pp. 225–37.
Stevenson, O. (1973), *Claimant or Client?* (London: Allen & Unwin).
Stevenson, O. (1976), 'Report to DHSS on action research project', unpublished monograph.
Stevenson, O. (1978), 'Reception into care – a case example in good enough parenting' (London: CCETSW).
Stroud, J. (1960), *The Shorn Lamb* (London: Longman).
Taylor, Carly, Report (1980), *Report on Carly Taylor* (Leicester: Leicestershire County Council).
Thomas, D., and Shaftoe, H. (1974), 'The patch system – does casework need a neighbourhood orientation?', *Social Work Today*, vol. 5, no. 16, pp. 483–6.
Thomas, D., and Warburton, R. (1977), *Community Workers in a Social Services Department – A Case Study* (London: Personal Social Services Council/National Institute for Social Work).
Tillich, P. (1952), *The Courage to Be* (London: Fontana).
Timms, N. (1964), *Psychiatric Social Work in Great Britain 1939–1962* (London: Routledge & Kegan Paul).
Timms, N. (1964), *Social Casework* (London: Routledge & Kegan Paul).
Timms, N. (1968), *The Language of Social Casework* (London: Routledge & Kegan Paul).
Towle, C. (1954), *The Learner in Education for the Professions* (Chicago: University of Chicago Press).
Towle, C. (1956), *Generic Trends in Education for Social Work* (London: Association of Social Workers).
Valencia, M., and Jackson, B. (1979), *Financial Aid Through Social Work* (London: Routledge & Kegan Paul).

Vickery, A. (1977), 'Social work practice: divisions and unifications', in H. Specht and A. Vickery (eds), *Integrating Social Work Practice* (London: Allen & Unwin).

Volunteer Centre (1976), *Creative Partnerships, A Study in Leicestershire of Voluntary Community Involvement* (Berkhamsted, Herts: Volunteer Centre).

Webb, A., and Hobdell, M. (1980), 'Co-ordination and teamwork in the health and personal social services' in Lonsdale *et al.*, pp. 97–110.

Williams Report (1967), *Caring for People* (London: Allen & Unwin).

Winnicott, C. (1955), 'Casework techniques in the child care service', reprinted in Younghusband (1966), pp. 135–54.

Winnicott, C. (1964), *Child Care and Social Work* (Welwyn, Herts: Codicote Press).

Younghusband Report (1959), *Report of the Working Party on Social Workers in the Local Authority Health and Welfare Services* (London: HMSO).

Younghusband, E. (ed.) (1966), *New Developments in Casework* (London: Allen & Unwin).

Younghusband, E. (1978), *Social Work in Britain 1950–1975* (London: Allen & Unwin).

Index

accountability 107
accreditation 55, 148
Acts of Parliament: Children (1975) 97; Children & Young Persons (1963) 117, (1969) 97; Chronically Sick & Disabled Persons (1970) 40, 117; Social Services (1970) 45
adolescents 43, 45, 46, 58, 62, 90, 132
adoption and fostering 61, 63, 96, 100
aids and adaptations 117
alcoholism 90
Allen, R., *see* Heywood, J.
assessment 82, 87, 93, 134
Association of: British Adoption . . . Agencies 97; Psychiatric Social Workers 39-40
attachment 33, 43, 74, 77-8, 79
Auckland Report 37, 152
Ausubel, D. 24, 152

Bartlett, H. M. 21-2, 23-4, 152
Batley, R. 121, 152
battered wives 58
bereavement 25, 26, 88, 92, 134
Biestek, F. 32, 152
Bowlby, J. 26, 152
Brent 101
Briggs, T. L. 78, *see also* Lonsdale, S.
British: Association of Social Workers 20, 30-1, 34; Medical Association 39
Browne, E. T. 61, 152
Bucher, R. 50, 122, 152
Bulmer, M. 65, 153
Butrym, Z. 14-15, 21, 76, 152
Bywaters, P. 20, 69, 152

caring network 73, 107
case conferences 78-9
Central: Council for Education & Training in Social Work 11, 31, 32, 123, 125, 135, 150, 152; Training Council in Child Care 31
centralisation 71
Certificate: in Social Service 21, 58, 124, 126, 135, 138-9; of Qualification in Social Work 124, 125, 126, 138-9, 140, 145, 147

child: abuse 38, 40, 51, 54, 58, 74, 78, 83, 119, 146-7; care 29, 31, 32, 33-4, 38, 61, 91, 93-5; guidance 80, 103; minders 80; problems 89
children('s): departments 137; deprived 33; non-accidental injury and deaths of 16, 37-8, 40, 45
Citizens' Advice Bureaux 116
Colwell, Maria 37-8, 152
common core 27, 28
communication 79-83
community: care 16-17, 40, 91, 119-21, 130, 135-6; work & workers 46, 69-70, 99, 119-21, 141, 142
confidentiality 68
Conservative Party 66
consultancy 150
consultation 76, 128
Cooper, J. 101, 152
co-operation, interprofessional 16, 36, 74-7, 77-9, 79-81, 83
co-ordination 36-9, 54, 74, 76, 81, 91, 94, 133, 149
courses 29, 31, 33, 35, 135, 138, 145, 147
courts 43, 83, 132, 143; civil 55; crown 80; juvenile 77; magistrates' 80
Coventry Community Development Project 121, 152
crisis work 87-90, 141
Currie, R. 22, 69, 70-4, 75, 91-2, 116, 152

day care 100, 128
deaf people 46, 61, 63, 98
delinquency 54, 129, 132
Department of Health & Social Security 11, 59n, 92, 117
deprivation 15
disabled people 117
divorce 25
doctors 48, 51, 79, *see also* General Practitioners
Dundee University 18-19, 153
Durkheim, E. 50
duty 85-7, 140

education and training 13, 19, 20, 31, 137-51

education welfare officers 37, 38, 78, 80
Edwards, J. *see* Batley, R.
emergency duty 99
emotional: disturbance 91, 101; involvement 68
Epstein, L. 86, *see also* Reid, W. J.
Essex 100
expertise: administrative and managerial 113; interaction 127-8; need for 55; notion 48-59; special 144; status of 69; types of 48
'Exshire' 120-1

family: advice centres 116; and child care 90-1; interaction theory 126; problems 36, 37, 40, 49, 83, 88, 115, 119, 132; Service Units 16, 42, 89-90, 103, 141; therapy 99; violence 58, 90
fields of practice 16, 28
fuel poverty 118

General: Nursing Council 123; practitioners, medical 15, 19, 51, 53, 80, 94, 98, 143
generic(ism) 13-16, 20-1
geriatrics 52, 114, 149
Glampson, A. 69, 153
Godfrey, Lisa 37, 38-9, 153
Goldberg, A. M. 45, 72-3, 76, 77, 82-3, 86-7, 89-90, 104, 114, 153
Goldstein, H. 18-19, 21, 153
group work 57, 103
Guardian, The 124

Hadley, R. 65-7, 153
Hall, A. 85, 153
Hallett, C. 16, 38, 153, *see also* Stevenson, O.
Halsey, A. H. 65, 153
handicap 54, 61, 72, 82, 92, 123
Harlesden Community Work Project 69-70, 153
health: centres 43, 77; departments 137; visitors 37, 61, 80, 94, 114
Heywood, J. 117, 153
Hill, M. 106, 115, 117, 153
hire purchase 118, 143
Hobdell, M. 74, 75, *see also* Webb, A.
Hollis, F. 32, 153
Holme, A. 107, 108, 153
Home Office 31, 153
hospital social work(ers) 16-17, 77, 80, 124, 150

housing officials 37, 80
Hunt, A. 33, 153
Hutchings, J. 103, 154

information 69-71, 76, 81, 119
Ingleby Committee 36, 154
Institute for Medical Social Work 31
intake 46, 63, 69, 86
integrated methods 69
intermediate treatment 47, 96, 128
International Congress on Child Abuse 51
interviewing 85
Irvine, E. 33, 154

Jackson, B. See Valencia, M.
Jay Report 122-4, 154
Jeans, M. 76, 154
Jordan, W. 117, 154

Kane, R. 78, 154
Keele University 59n, 72
key worker 42, 95
knowledge: base of sound 21, 150; 'explosion' 51, 55; extent required for current problems 53; fragmentation of 21, 22

Laing, P. 115, *see also* Hill, M.
Lambert, L., *see* Rowe, J.
landlords 80, 118
law 52, 55, 66, 89, 114, 146
leisure 106
London School of Economics 29, 31
long-term casework 89, 109
Lonsdale, S. 78, 154
loss 25-6, 88

McGrath, M. See Hadley, R.
Maizells, J. See Holme, A.
Malherbe, M. 30, 55, 154
Marris, P. 26, 154
Mattinson, J. 42, 88-90, 154
medical: officers of health 113; profession 66, 111, 113; social workers 31-2, 34; specialists 52, 53
mental: handicap 40, 61, 72, 73, 101, 122, 123; illness 40, 90, 111, 122, 143; welfare officers 38
methods of work 16, 28
Meurs, S. 37, 154
Meyer, C. 115-16, 154
Minahan, A., *see* Pincus, A.

Index

Moore, W. E. 154
multiple visiting 137

National: Association of Probation Officers 30-1; Health Service 34, 40, 78, 123; Joint Committee 64; Society for the Prevention of Cruelty to Children 16, 37, 42
Neill, J. 77-8. See also Goldberg, E. M.
nurses 111, 122, 123-4

occupational therapists 46, 114
old people 43, 52, 83, 91, 92, 93, 107, 124, 193
one-parent families 46
Open University, The 147

Packman, J. 21, 32, 154
Parad, J. 88, 154
Parker, R. 74-5, 80-1, 154
Parkes, C. M. 26, 154
Parrott, B., *see* Currie, R.
Parsloe, P. 12, 48, 69-70, 74-5, 84, 129, 154
patch system 64-74, 116
Peacock, S. 37, 154
Perlman, H. 32, 154
physical disability 62, 72, 73, 92
Pincus, A. 18, 21, 154
placement 140-4
police 80, 83
practice wisdom 60-1
Presthus, R. 57, 154
preventive work 80
Probation: courses 31; national association 30-1; service 103, 104, 106; students 34
professional: conduct 55; identity 29, 122; mystique 66; standards 75; unification 29-31
psychiatric: community nurses 111; social workers 29, 32, 78
psychiatrists 78, 112
psychologists 61, 103

Rapoport, R. N. 111-12, 154
receptionist 85, 118
referral 79, 81, 85
Reid, W. J. 86, 154
research 11n, 23, 53, 70, 71, 83, 85, 86, 90, 92, 114, 150
residential care 31, 68, 121-30, 136, 149
Rowbottom, R. 53-4, 154

Rowe, J. 154
Rowlings, C. 85, 86, 92, 155
rural-urban contrast 64

'safety net' 116-17
Sainsbury, E. 103-6, 109-10, 119-20, 155
school medical officers 37
schools 74, 77, 80, 124-5
Scotland 13n, 38
'Seatown' 45, 76, 83, 87, 104
Seebohm Report 13, 33, 35-47, 58, 101, 113, 128, 155
segments 50, 56
self-help groups 73
service, direct and indirect 23
settings 16
Shaftoe, H. 67-9
short-term work 86, 87-9, 128
Shyne, A. W. 86, *see also* Reid, W. J.
Sinclair, I. *see* Mattinson, J.
social security 115, 117
Social Services: departments 11, 18, 22-3, 42, 49, 57, 62, 63, 103, 112-14, 115, 116-18; records 70; Study Groups 86, 155
social work(ers): advice and help function 114-19, 130; assistants 134-5; career grade 55-6; director 113; education 70, 72; field 127; graduate 119; group status 78; hospital and medical 16-17, 31, 77, 80, 124, 150; role 114, 115; salaries 64; staff development 147-9, 150, 151; wrongly regarded as psychotherapists 76, *see also* specialisation.
solicitors 83
Specht, H. 155
specialisation: analogues 51-3, 59; and ideological commitment 112; and risk 64; as division of work 50; as reaction to generic work 71-2; as special expertise 50; by method 119-21; client-group 35, 44; determinants 63-4; disadvantages of 57-8; 'felt need' for 95-101; in area teams 130-6, 144; in crisis work 89; informal 44, 45-6, 47, 57, 59, 63, 72; in health-care teams 92; in residential work 122, 130, 149; in social security 117; in sub-teams 93; 'level three' 149; organisational 45, 46, 57; practitioner level 46; teams 84-5
special schools 124-5
staff development 40, 147, 150, 151

Standing Conference of Organizations of Social Workers 30
status 78, 125, 126
stereotypes 30
Stevenson, O. 22, 38, 45, 61, 73, 79, 81, 106, 153, *see also* Hallett, C., Hill, M.
Strauss, A., *see* Bucher, R.
street wardens 67, 141
stress 24
Stroud, J. 32, 155
suicide attempts 88
Supplementary Benefits 79, 81; Commission 105-6; officials 79, 106, 115, 116-17

Tavistock Clinic 33
Taylor, Carly 38-9, 155
teachers and teaching profession 51-2, 76, 110, 114, 124, 137
teams: area 95-101, 112, 114, 120, 132-4, 150; core 93-4; district handicap 93; extended 94; health-care 92; hospital 93; insularity of 149; intake 87; organisation 132, 149-50; structure 84-95; support 94, 95
therapeutic community 111-12
Thomas, D. 67-9, 120-1, 155
Tillich, P. 155
Timms, N. 14-15, 21, 32, 33, 155
Towle, C. 20-1, 23, 32, 33, 155
training: Certificate in Social Service 58; councils 139; in-service 56, 139, 148; joint 123; preliminary 135; psychiatric social work 32; 'workshops' 149
transfer of knowledge or skills 21, 34

travelling expenses 64
trigger factors 90

unemployment 25, 79, 106, 114, 117
United States of America: 'direct/indirect' debate 23-4; influence 32-3, 122; methods of intervention 17; specialisation debate 13; terminology 16
universities 31, 32, 59, 72, 147

Valencia, M. 117, 155
Vickery, A. 17, 18, 19, 23-4, 69, 156, *see also* Specht, H.
visual handicap 46, 98
voluntary agencies 33, 80, 107, 118, 122, 123, 142
Volunteer Centre 108, 156

Wales 65, 103
Wandsworth 101
Warburton, R. 45, 72-3, 76, 77, 82-3, 86-7, 89-90, 104, 120-1, *see also* Goldberg, E. M., Thomas, D.
Webb, A. 74-5, 78, 156, *see also* Lonsdale, S.
Wedge, P., *see* Cooper, J.
welfare rights 112, 118
Williams Report 125, 127-8, 156
Winnicott, C. 33, 156

Younghusband, E. 13, 29, 31, 32, 125, 156
youth: and community work 98; workers 144